JAZZ HARP.

By Richard Hunter.

Oak Publications
New York/London/Sydney/Cologne

For Patty and Little Walter, who met in a dream.

Special thanks to Mr. Krasilovsky.

Acknowledgements

I would like to thank a few people for their help in putting this book together. First, my wife Patty, who suggested the book in the first place, and has since typed, edited, read, and reread, offered support, and done all the other things I could possibly ask of my favorite human.
Next, my mother, who did her share in helping to get a certain publisher interested in my book on jazz harp styles.
Finally, thanks to Jason Shulman, whose suggestions have always been useful and to the point.

Edited by Halley Gatenby
Music edited by Peter Pickow

International Standard Book Number: 0.8256.0229.7
Library of Congress Catalog Card Number: 79-92155

Exclusive Distributors:
Music Sales Corporation
225 Park Avenue South, New York, NY 10003
Music Sales Limited
8/9 Frith Street, London W1V 5TZ England
Music Sales Pty. Limited
120 Rothschild Street, Rosebery, Sydney, NSW 2018, Australia

Printed in the United States of America by
Vicks Lithograph and Printing Corporation

Contents

Introduction

Until recently, jazz has been an idiom largely neglected by harp players, for several reasons. First, there haven't been many players with the technical ability needed to play modern jazz, and until very recently most people with that ability were interested pretty exclusively in classical styles. In addition, the harp itself is not designed in a way that makes jazz easy to play. Jazz requires a smooth, legato attack, and accents in a jazz line can fall on any part of the beat. It's hard to play the harp legato because of constant breath shifts, and even harder to accent freely. That's why some very skilled harp players have said that they doubt that it's possible to play jazz on the harp.

I don't agree. It's true that you can't play the harp the way Coltrane played the tenor sax, as Toots Thielemans has said. And it would be very hard to play the harp the way Charlie Parker played his horn. But that doesn't put the harp out of the running. Coltrane and Parker didn't say it all. If harp players can't play jazz like sax players, then they'll have to play their own kind of jazz, just as blues harp players play their own kind of blues.

The time is right for harp players to take that step. Jazz is wide open to new sounds and influences, more so than ever before. Musicians who wouldn't touch anything but bebop as recently as five or ten years ago are now recording Stevie Wonder tunes and using electronic instruments.

Harp players, too, seem to be edging closer to jazz from many different directions. Players like Norton Buffalo and Stevie Wonder, using techniques that come more or less easily to the harp, especially the chromatic, are chipping away more and more boldly at the limits of a harp style defined, on the one hand, by pop players like the Harmonicats, and on the other by blues harpists. The role of the harp in improvised music is being redefined on terms set by harp players and composers themselves.

I don't mean to say that harp players going into jazz can afford to ignore Parker, Coltrane, Ellington, Armstrong, et al. But jazz harp is not just jazz, it's *harp*. Learn what the great jazz players have done, but don't forget that there are a lot of great sounds that can only come out of a harp. Listen to blues players for their wild tones. Listen to classical players for their incredible tone control and chord chops, and listen to jazz players for their ability to instantaneously create melody out of some of the most difficult material imaginable.

Most harp players don't know enough about the people who play the harp in styles outside their own. Believe me, there've been plenty of great players, and most of them sound very different from one another. Listen to recordings by Little Walter, Big Walter Horton, both Sonny Boy Williamsons, Stevie Wonder, Larry Adler, Blackie Schackner, George Fields, Toots Thielemans, John Sebastian Sr., Chamber Huang. Know your horn: Pump people who know more than you do for all they're worth.

When the artificial barriers that exist between different harp styles come down, and harp players take it on themselves to learn their axes as well as sax players know theirs, we'll see a real explosion in improvised harp styles. You can be part of it. Learn your horn, keep your ears open, and practise, practise, practise. Jazz harp is on the way—get to work now and you'll be on time for that train.

How to Use This Book

Most people who read this book will probably be either blues harp or pop players, with perhaps a few classical types checking it out for curiosity's sake. Of these, the only ones who've done much jamming will probably be the blues harpists. They have an advantage in the sense that they're willing to experiment and already know a bit about the rhythms of black music. But the blues is much simpler, in terms of chord changes and rhythms, than jazz, and most blues players will have to work hard on their technique to become good jazz players.

Learning to play jazz may take years of playing and study, but the rewards are so great that people who are serious about their music can't afford not to try. The first thing any harp player who wants to play jazz should do is learn to play the chromatic. It's an ornery beast, and not as loud or flexible as the Marine Band, but you can't really play complex chord patterns without it. The way the Marine Band is set up, you can't get all twelve chromatic notes in every octave, even with bends and overblows. As long as you stick to one scale, or a few related chords, fine, but most jazz doesn't. Don't drop the blues harp, though. There are plenty of things you *can* do with it, as we'll see later on.

When you start to play the chromatic, begin by picking out scales—major, minor, diminished, pentatonic, and so on—and arpeggios, just to get a feel for the way it's set up. (If some of these terms are hanging you up, better get a pocket musical dictionary.) You'll find lots of scales and arpeggios numbered for the chrom at the end of this book. Try out some melodies, simple or tough, whatever you can handle. My next piece of advice means a lot of work, but is essential: Transpose everything—yes, everything—you play into all twelve keys. The days are long gone when jazz players only had to play in B♭. Once you know all your scales, it'll be much easier. There's information on transposing techniques elsewhere in this book.

Once you have some knowledge of the chromatic, go out and find yourself a good teacher who can show you how to breathe right, and can get you working on techniques that will polish your tone and articulation. It's sad but true that there aren't many harp players around who are good enough to teach jazz. So it might even be a good idea to find a sax or trumpet teacher who can show you how to breathe and teach you about jazz phrasing. I've loaded this book with information about specific harp techniques, but you need someone to listen to you as much as you need to look at exercises and transcriptions.

When you pick this book up, skim the whole thing first. Take a look at the transcriptions, dig the various exercises, and read the technical information to get a feel for what's here. The transcriptions are arranged mostly in increasing order of difficulty. Each harp solo has been chosen because it shows off a particular harp style. The horn solos illustrate certain approaches to improvisation that don't exist in the recorded harp music that I've heard.

Always listen to the record while you look at the transcription—it'll make the notation much easier to understand. When you read the text that goes with each solo, you'll see a lot of specific measure references. Follow them up, *after* you've listened to the solo; otherwise you may wonder what all the fuss is about.

It's impossible to deal thoroughly with a subject like jazz in a volume this size—John Mehegan filled well over 1000 pages in the *Jazz Improvisation* series—so many important ideas and subjects are only mentioned in passing. Following are a few suggestions about ways to supplement the material in this book in order to develop a stronger jazz conception.

To play jazz you need a fair knowledge of theory. You can get this from a teacher, from books, at school, or by divine gift. (Is your name Mozart?) You'll have to know something about voice leading; learn a few cadences; learn what various chord types are and how they relate to each other. You'll also need a look at the specific kinds of voicings that jazz players use on various chord types. The bibliography at the end of this book has information on where to find this stuff, and also lists some good exercise books written for other instruments, but useful for harp.

Jazz, like classical music or blues, has an established repertoire, and you'll need to know at least some of it. Get your hands on some fake books, which give the melody of a tune and chord symbols, and learn the tunes of Duke Ellington, Charlie Parker, Miles Davis, John Coltrane, Thelonious Monk, and any other composers you like. Somewhere along the line you're probably going to have to learn to read music. People make such a big deal out of reading, and it's a sore point with so many players, that I am relieved to report that it's not anywhere near as difficult as climbing Mt. Everest or making 10th Dan Black Belt. Of course, it's not easy to read a page of an orchestral score at sight, but with enough regular practice anyone should be able to read simple melodies. Remember: set a beat, very slow if necessary, and *stick to it*. Keep reading ahead of what you're playing, and don't stop until the piece ends. That way you'll get at least the general outline of what you're playing. One of the main reasons for learning to read is to pick up ideas and forms quickly.

Whenever you get the chance, play jazz: Play with people who are better than you, or play along with records. Listen carefully to solos, and figure out what's happening in passages that catch your ear. Jazz is group music, so play with a group, or whomever you find that can cut it.

Jazz is a new area of exploration for harp players, with only one recognized hero so far—Toots Thielemans—and lots of tantalizing bits and pieces to make up the barest foundation of a tradition. I'm sure that the best is still waiting to be played, and I hope that it's your good luck to play it. This book will serve as an introduction to a few jazz styles. Open your ears and heart and create some music of your own.

A Few Things About Chords

I don't want to spend too much time on a detailed discussion of harmony, but I feel it important to discuss a few chord types. We'll use chords that can be found on either the Marine Band or chromatic harps, so those of you who don't know any piano or guitar won't have to wait until you learn those instruments to get something out of it.

All chords are constructed of thirds (in diatonic harmony, anyway, which is what almost all jazz is about). The simplest kind of chord is a *triad*: This is a three-note chord consisting of a *root*, a third above the root; and another third above that (a fifth above the root). It's easy to think of a triad as just every other note of a major scale. There are four types of triads: *major, minor, augmented,* and *diminished.* Since any type of triad can be built on any given root, the type of triad is determined by what kind of 3rd and 5th are in the chord.

A *major triad* has a major 3rd and a perfect 5th. On the piano, using C as the root, it looks like this:

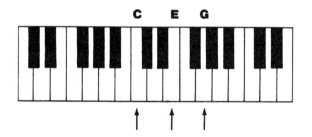

On the Marine Band, blow on holes 1-2-3 or 4-5-6 for this triad.

A *minor triad* has a minor 3rd (lowered one half-step from major) and a perfect 5th. On the piano, again with C as the root, it looks like this:

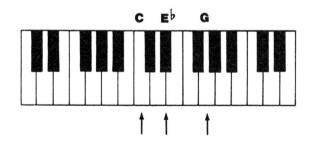

You can play a minor triad by drawing on holes 4-5-6 of any Marine Band.

A *diminished triad* has a minor 3rd and a diminished 5th (this means that the 5th is flatted). On the piano:

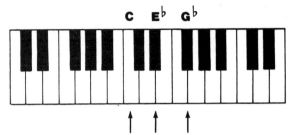

Play this triad by drawing on holes 3-4-5 on any Marine Band.

An *augmented triad* has a major 3rd and an augmented 5th (the 5th is raised one half-step). On the piano:

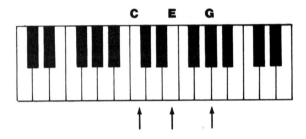

This triad can't be played on either the Marine Band or chromatic; but if you break the chord up into an arpeggio, it can be played on the chromatic, based on C, as follows:

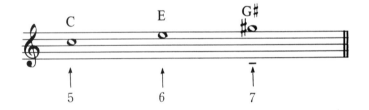

If we take any major scale—for now, we'll use the C major scale—and build a triad on each note of the scale, taking the 3rd and 5th of each triad from the same scale, we get the following:

Notice that triads built on the first, fourth, and fifth degrees of the scale are major (indicated by upper-case Roman numerals); triads built on the second, third, and sixth degrees of the scale are minor (indicated by lower-case Roman numerals); the triad built on the seventh degree of the scale is diminished. The augmented triad doesn't occur naturally in the major-scale-tone triads; however, it does occur in the triad built on the third degree of the harmonic minor scale.

Major and minor scales in twelve keys are listed for chrom at the back of this book.

Since there are only twelve different major keys (one for every note of the chromatic scale), and each major key contains three major and three minor triads, it's obvious that a given major or minor triad might belong to any one of three major keys. In an improvising situation, the scales used against a given chord will help to clarify the sense of the chord in terms of its relationship to a key center. For instance, using the notes of a C scale against a D minor triad will tend to identify the chord as ii of C, rather than i in D minor or vi in F major.

Jazz harmony is too complex, as a rule, for simple triads to be useful (except in pre-Armstrong styles), so jazz chords use higher intervals on top of the basic triads. These intervals are added on in thirds, just as the triads are constructed. The first addition is the *7th*, a 3rd above the 5th. There are three varieties of 7ths: major, minor, and diminished. The major 7th occurs naturally as the seventh degree of a major scale.

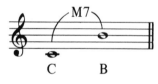

The minor 7th is a half-step below that.

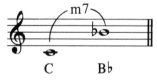

The diminished 7th is another half-step below the minor. It sounds the same as the sixth degree of the major scale.

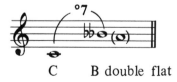

If we add a 7th to each of the major-scale-tone triads, we get:

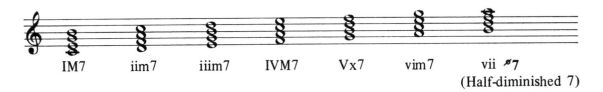

| IM7 | iim7 | iiim7 | IVM7 | Vx7 | vim7 | vii ♯7 |

(Half-diminished 7)

Now we have *Major 7th* chords (major 3rd, perfect 5th, major 7th) on the first and fourth degrees of the scale; a *Minor 7th* chord (minor 3rd, perfect 5th, minor 7th) on the second, third, and sixth degrees of the scale; a *Minor 7th with a flatted 5th* or *Half-diminished 7th* chord on the seventh degree of the scale (minor 3rd, diminished 5th, minor 7th); and a *Dominant 7th* chord (major 3rd, perfect 5th, minor 7th) on the fifth degree of the scale. Notice that the Dominant 7th chord contains the interval of a diminished 5th, or *tritone,* between its 3rd and 7th (B to F). The tritone is one of the most dissonant and unstable intervals; it conveys an element of tension and just doesn't sound "at rest" the way a perfect 5th does. Consequently, a chord containing a tritone will usually want to resolve to something more stable, like a major triad.

Now, to jump ahead a little bit, I'd like to point out that in tonal music the most powerful bass motion is up a perfect 4th or down a perfect 5th. When the Dominant 7th chord—the V^7 in any major key—moves to the *tonic,* or I chord, the bass moves either up a 4th or down a 5th. The diminished 5th within the Dominant 7th chord resolves—the 3rd up a half-step, and the 7th down a half-step—to the root and 3rd of the tonic chord. This kind of movement—from V^7 to I—is fundamental to tonal music, and is called a *cadence.* A cadence is usually defined as a harmonic formula that establishes a key center. There are many different kinds of cadences, but the V—I cadence is the granddaddy of them all. On the piano, in the key of C, it looks like:

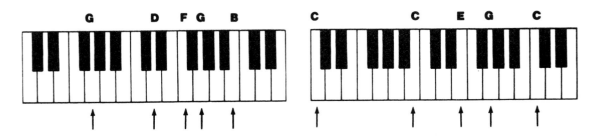

On a Marine Band, you can play a V^7 chord by drawing on holes 2-3-4-5; if you then blow on holes 1-2-3-4, you'll have played a V^7—I cadence, although the voice leading won't be exactly right.

Next look at the ii^7 chord. Here it is on the piano:

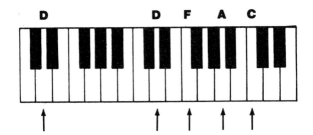

If we add ii[7] before the V[7], we get the most common cadence in jazz music. Notice that the bass motion from ii[7] to V[7] is up a perfect 4th. Notice also that the 7th of the ii[7] chord resolves to the 3rd of the V[7] chord, just as the 7th of the V[7] chord resolves to the 3rd of the tonic chord. In addition, the 3rd of the ii[7] becomes the 7th of the V[7].

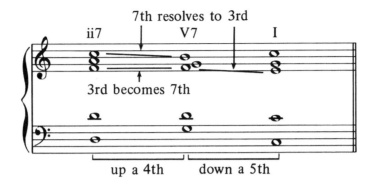

This is a very brief treatment of a complex subject. There are many different ways to relate the chords of one key to the chords of another. For those of my readers who don't know anything at all about theory and harmony, it would be a very good idea to learn all the scale-tone 7th chords in every key, and all the scales that go with those chords. In the back of this book, you'll find major, harmonic minor, diminished, and whole-tone scales in every key; and arpeggios (broken chords) for all the Major 7th, Minor 7th, Dominant 7th, and Diminished 7th chords, along with augmented triads (which go with whole-tone scales). Study those, and then, when you've really got some knowledge of functional harmony, you'll know how to construct lines that fit whatever chords you're faced with in a particular tune.

Harp Notation

Diatonic Harps
↑ = blow note
↓ = draw note
A bent tail ⌐ or ⌐ means bend the note. The tail will have one slash for every half-step of bend.

A small circle above the head of an arrow ↑ means overblow the note.

Chromatic Harps
↑ = blow note
↓ = draw note
A horizontal line above the head of a note ↑ or ↓ means push in the slide.
Bent tails and slashes have the same meaning as they do in diatonic notation.
A small circle above a hole number but below the arrow means the lowest octave on a 64.
(Look at your 64: that's the way it's numbered on the harp.)

First Steps: R&B Sax

Tom Scott: Raised on Robbery

This solo was originally played on the tenor sax, not the harp. It's important for harp players to listen to musicians who play other instruments, just as jazz guitarists and pianists cop licks from horn players. This is especially true because of the dearth of jazz harp players to learn from. If you want to base your style on the playing of more than a few guys, you'd better dig something besides the harp.

Analysis

This is an R&B piece, but Scott is a jazzman at heart and his lines have plenty of hip turns to them even in this simple setting. Pay special attention to Scott's rhythm; it's not too tough to play from a technical point of view, but people who're used to the blues may not hear it right away. Modern jazz and R&B, which are getting closer all the time, use different accenting from the blues. Blues players usually come down hard on the first half of a beat,

while jazz players tend to accent the weak half of the beat;

Notice how the accents fall in the third measure of Scott's solo.

He accents every third sixteenth note, imposing a triplet feel over the $\frac{4}{4}$ meter. Notice too how Scott uses sixteenth-note anticipations to push the rhythm in bars four and eight.

14

This sort of syncopation is common to jazz and R&B players, but not so everyday to blues. Also check out the emphasis on the weak half of either the first or second beat in bars five, six, and seven.

To get this kind of rhythmic flexibility into your playing, go over the exercises in the book in the following way.

First, play through the exercises with an even rhythm and attack. Then play them through again, accenting the first sixteenth note in each group of four:

Again, accenting the second sixteenth note,

and so on. When you've played them through with accents on each sixteenth note in turn, try accenting in odd groups—every third note in the exercise; every fifth note, etc.

When you can play a variety of accent patterns, try changing the rhythm of the exercises. Instead of:

you could play:

or

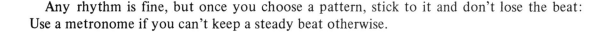

Any rhythm is fine, but once you choose a pattern, stick to it and don't lose the beat: Use a metronome if you can't keep a steady beat otherwise.

Throughout this book, you'll see rhythms and accent patterns that you'll never hear out of a blues band. Whatever you're playing, keep the basic pulse in your head—most jazz players tap their feet—and practise difficult passages over and over until you can match the sound and feel of the recording. Eventually your ears will pick up the sound of jazz articulations and the language of jazz rhythms. Memorize a lot of solos and Charlie Parker tunes and it'll be sooner.

Scott basically plays with two ideas in this piece, both of them having to do with approaches to C, the tonic note. The first idea is an approach from above; E descends to D and then to C. The second idea is an approach from below; G rises to A, then to C. (These notes, by the way, together make up a pentatonic scale, about which more later.) He alternates these two ideas, moving them up or down an octave for emphasis, to give the solo a simple but effective balance. The E-D-C motif is used in measures one-two, four, and seven-eight; the G-A-C motif takes up measures three and five (where it provides the climax) and the lead-in.

Notice the back-and-forth motion between C and D in the fourth measure:

This kind of over and under approach to a note is characteristic of jazz solos of any era.

Harp How-To

This piece isn't too hard on either the Marine Band or the chromatic, but watch out for a few things. First, on the Marine Band, the E♭ in bar seven can only be played with an overblow. Overblowing is discussed in more detail in the section, *Modern Harp Technique*. Basically, it's a lot like bending in the upper register, but the reed pops up to the harmonic instead of flattening down. The blow 6 reed on an F Marine Band won't overblow easily; if you have a lot of trouble, substitute draw 7 for the overblow.

In bar three, get those rhythms right, and play the notes loud and clear, with hard tonguing to push the beat. Many blues harp players have a poor sound on their blow notes, because the blues is mostly low register draw notes. Breathe evenly from your gut, and don't settle for a weak tone: that middle register has a lot of power.

Hit the G-A-C line in the fifth bar hard and clean. There are no bends involved, so there should be no problem if you practise carefully. The eighth note rest at the beginning of the bar gives you plenty of time to jump from the last note of measure four.

When you play this, you'll use the whole harp, from top to bottom, instead of just a few notes at each end. The *whole harp;* it's all there, you might as well use it. The ability to play smoothly from one end of the harp to the other will open up many alternatives to the bottom-oriented lines into which most blues harpists are locked. Check out the scales and exercises after the solo.

Knock yourself out now. Keep it clean.

Raised on Robbery

Joni Mitchell

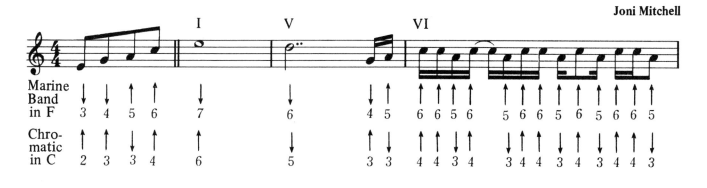

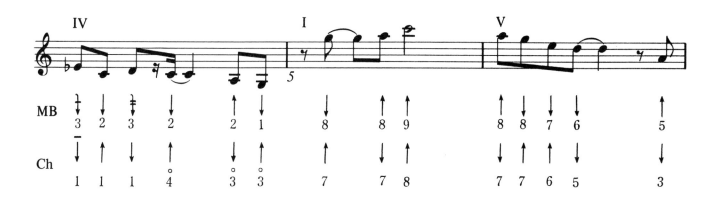

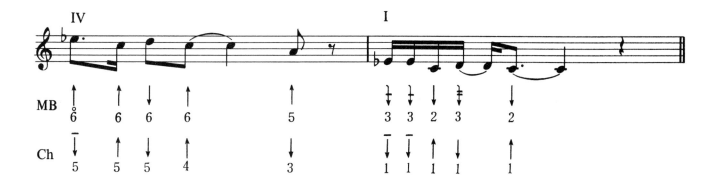

Bending exercises

Marine Band in C

Arpeggios

Scale exercise

Supplementary Discography

Tom Cat – Tom Scott and the L.A. Express (out of print)
  Great jazz-rock with emphasis on the *rock*. Many of Scott's tunes, like "Rock Island Rocket," can be played on the Marine Band.

Blow It Out – Tom Scott and the L.A. Express (Epic/Ode PE-34966)
  More jazz-rock.

Wrap Around Joy – Carole King (Epic/Ode PE-34953)
  The tune "Jazz Man" has excellent, screaming R&B sax by Tom Scott that also works on the blues harp. Of course, you can play any of these tunes on the chrom, but because the Marine Band has a heavier tone, it is more suitable for some R&B styles.

Structure in Jazz Tunes

Jazz is a lot more complex, rhythmically and harmonically, than the blues. This is true partly because the blues is a folk music, while jazz is an art music that draws on many different sources, including the blues. Following is a look at the way some types of jazz tunes are put together.

Maybe the easiest way to get into structure is to see how a jazz blues might differ from a folk blues by Little Walter or Sonny Terry, for example. As most blues players know, the basic twelve-bar blues is made up of three chords, I, IV, and V. In the key of F, those chords are F, B♭, and C, respectively.

$$\begin{array}{cccccccccccc} \text{I} & \text{I} & \text{I} & \text{IV} & \text{IV} & \text{I} & \text{I} & \text{V} & \text{IV} & \text{I} & \text{I} \\ \frac{4}{4}\ \text{F} & \text{F} & \text{F} & \text{B♭} & \text{B♭} & \text{F} & \text{F} & \text{C} & \text{B♭} & \text{F} & \text{F} \end{array}$$

This is pretty simple stuff and, since it's all thoroughly grounded in F, most blues players wouldn't even think about chord changes. They'd concentrate instead on simple melodies or riffs whose rhythms might accent the chord changes, but whose pitches wouldn't necessarily support those changes. In the head choruses of Little Walter's "Juke" and "Backtrack," for instance, you can see clearly that he's working off the rhythm, not the harmony.

In a jazz blues, the harmony is more complex. Here's an example of a harmonization of a Charlie Parker blues:

$$\begin{array}{cccccccc} \text{I VI} & \text{II} & \text{V} & \text{I} & \text{Vm} & \text{Ix}^7 & \text{IVx}^7 & \text{♯IV}^\text{o} \\ \frac{4}{4}\ \text{F Dm}^7 & \text{Gm}^7\ \text{C}^7 & \text{F} & & \text{Cm}^7\ \text{F}^7 & \text{B♭}^7 & \text{Bdim}^7 \end{array}$$

$$\begin{array}{cccccccc} \text{V+}^6\ \text{IV} & \text{III} & \text{VIx}^7\ \text{II} & \text{V} & \text{I VI} & \text{II} & \text{V} \\ \text{C+}^6\ \text{B♭ m}^7 & \text{Am}^7\ \text{D}^7 & \text{Gm}^7 & \text{C}^7 & \text{F Dm}^7 & \text{Gm}^7 & \text{C}^7 \end{array}$$

Let's take this a little bit at a time so you can make some sense out of all these changes. First off, notice the pattern in the first two measures:

$$\begin{array}{cccc} \text{I VI} & \text{II} & \text{V} \\ \frac{4}{4}\ \text{F Dm}^7 & \text{Gm}^7 & \text{C}^7 \end{array}$$

The last part of this cadence, II-V, (in F, G Minor to C^7), is the single most common cadence in jazz. In the first three bars, Parker establishes F as his key center. In bar four, the chords C Minor-F^7 (II-V in the key of B♭), set up the arrival of the B♭ chord in bar five, which is then held for a full measure to emphasize this *new* center. The B Diminished chord in bar six leads up to the C+^{6} chord in measure seven. The A Minor-D^7 pattern in bar eight sets up the G Minor chord in bar nine (A Minor-D^7 is II-V cadence in the key of G), which then becomes part of a two-measure, II-V cadence in F (G Minor-C^7) leads us back to F in bar eleven.

20

This may sound confusing, but if you look closely you'll see that the II-V patterns lead you to chords that function as strong key centers within the twelve-bar pattern. The repetition of the II-V pattern in bars eight and ten—first A Minor-D^7, then G Minor-C^7—is a fine example of a *sequence*, an important device in many jazz tunes.

Harmonic rhythm, or the duration of specific chords and key centers, also helps to emphasize the importance of an arrival on a specific chord. The best example here is the two-bar cadence, G Minor-C^7, that makes the arrival of F in bar eleven seem so final. Notice that this is the longest cadence in the piece.

It may take a while to completely understand this kind of harmonic thinking. The main point is that, in jazz, you don't just arrive slam-bang at some chord and then jump off to the next. Changes of harmony are prepared, and every chord either is a temporary key center, or helps to set one up. Knowing which scales go with which chords makes it easier to bring in chord changes clearly, without confusing the tonality. For instance, look at bar four of our Parker blues. Knowing that both C Minor and F^7 can be outlined with modes of a B♭ scale helps to make the arrival of the B♭ chord in measure five more convincing.

To repeat: In the folk blues, melody is supreme, and harmony has no function. In jazz, harmony usually dictates melody, so the relative weight of a chord—its duration and function—is very important.

Other Forms in Jazz

Jazz players work out on many different types of material, not just blues. In the last five or ten years there has been a real explosion in jazz as sources of ideas that previously were considered not worth tapping—especially rock—have entered the mainstream. In this space it's impossible to sum up all the types of structures that jazz players now use, but I'll try to describe a few of the more common forms.

Until the middle 1960s most jazz was played on standard tunes that were either created by jazz composers like Duke Ellington or Billy Strayhorn, or taken from popular or Broadway show music. These tunes were usually made up of thirty-two bars divided into four eight-bar sections. Often the first, second, and fourth eight-bar sections were the same, while the third eight-bar unit (the bridge) had a different melodic and harmonic structure. This is an AABA structure. Some tunes that have this form include Gershwin's "I Got Rhythm," Ellington's "Satin Doll" and "Take the A Train," Parker's "Scrapple From the Apple" and "Dexterity," Dizzy Gillespie's "A Night In Tunisia," and Miles Davis's "So What" (transcribed later in this book).

Variations on the thirty-two-bar form include ABAC, where the first and third sections are the same and the second and fourth are different; and ABCD, where each eight-bar section is different. The important thing about all of these forms is that they repeat every thirty-two bars, and each thirty-two-bar unit is made up of eight-bar sections.

Another type of tune has little or no repetition from beginning to end, although the entire form may be repeated any number of times in performance. John Coltrane's "Giant Steps" and Mingus's "Goodbye Pork Pie Hat" are two examples. These tunes usually have internal phrasing that breaks down into regular units, but the tunes are not made up of repeating blocks of melody.

In the early 1960s, jazz players began to abandon chord changes as the basis for improvisation. Players like Ornette Coleman cut loose from diatonic harmony altogether, although their song forms might still be based on repeating phrases of a given number of measures. John Coltrane made landmark recordings of "My Favorite Things" and "Summertime" which after a brief statement of the melody, featured long solos over repeated two-chord vamps. Miles Davis, in *Bitches Brew, Jack Johnson,* and later recordings, structured his tunes on rhythmic motifs and ensemble textures rather than any repeating harmonic scheme. Today, in the late seventies, people involved in New York's loft scene are producing pieces whose forms are so complex that many musicians can't understand them at first hearing. (And you should see the notation for that stuff!)

Remember, though, that most jazz is built on a repeating chord structure, just like the blues. The differences are, first, that the repeating structures are usually longer in jazz, and second, that within those forms the harmony is always moving to specific points of climax and resolution. It's your job, as a harp player, to find those points of resolution and make them convincing. There are many ways to do it—swing players do it with blues lines, and bop players use forms that are almost baroque. Most of these forms are built on repetition, and by listening you can learn to hear those structures in your head, just as you learned to hear a twelve-bar blues. When you can match your knowledge of scales and harmony to forms, you can create your own melodies on these patterns. At that point, you're beginning to play jazz.

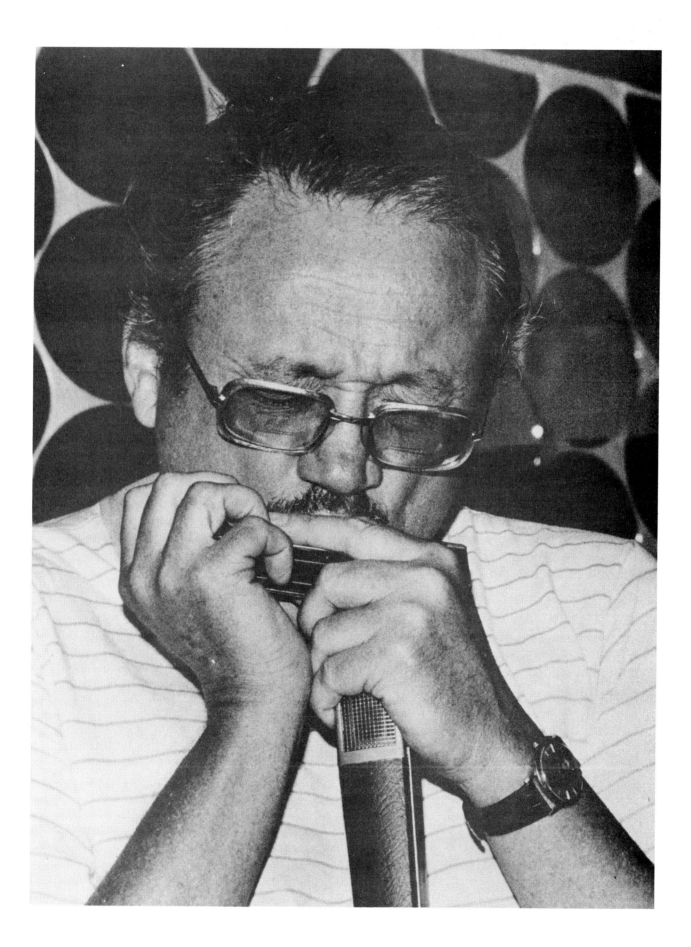

The Master at Work

Toots Thielemans: What Becomes of Your Life

Toots Thielemans is the only widely known harp player who can truly be called a *jazz* harp player. He plays bebop, ballads, and modern modal jazz with style and control, even at very quick tempos. He can create fine melodies on all sorts of material, as he's proved many times over in his solos and compositions.

Toots's style, as you'd expect from a man who began his career in bebop, is horn oriented. He almost never plays octaves or chords—an exception is the minor 2nds he plays on Joanne Brackeen's tune "Snooze," on the *Captured Alive* LP, by pushing the slide halfway in on the chrom. (When you push the slide in halfway, you get the C and C♯ scales simultaneously.) Toots rarely plays Marine Band, and he seems to be totally uninfluenced by the great blues players. His tone is light, with a very mild, slow vibrato. He never uses the gutty throat vibrato of the Chicago players, and he doesn't use an amp to change the basic tone of the harp.

Toots is at his best in a ballad setting, where his clear singing tone sounds as pure as the air in heaven. Like Stevie Wonder, he has a lot of little runs that he works with the slide. "I Never Told You, " from Quincy Jones's *Walking In Space,* is a particularly beautiful example of this technique.

Analysis

"What Becomes of Your Life" is a good introduction to Toots's ballad work. The solo isn't as tough as a lot of his music. The key of D major lets him use some quick licks that sound great but aren't too hard to play. The D-B-A lick in measure five is one example. The notes here are all draw, so the only problem is the jump from A (draw 7) to D (draw 9), a minor difficulty at worst. The similar line in measure nine is only a little harder, mainly because of the jump to F at the end of the bar. Hit the F (draw 10) hard; it's the high point of the solo in more ways than one. The falling line that follows shouldn't be any problem: There are no jumps, and almost all the notes are draw. Dig the pattern of draw slide in, draw slide out, down a hole and do it again: very Toots.

The way Toots uses bends is essential to his style. The rising chromatic line beginning in bar seven gains a lot of power from the bending that makes the line sound like a continuous upward curve. Also, Toots never accents a note with heavy vibrato; instead he often uses a slow, heavy bend to give a note soul. Examples are in bars one, nine, and ten (listen to the record). Bend on a chromatic the way you do on a Marine Band, but don't punch it too hard, or the note will blank out or jump to a harmonic. Starting a note straight and then bringing in the bend gives a nice sound, and makes it easier to avoid blankouts. Just about every note on a chrom will bend, which is more than you can say for a blues harp.

Check out the overall structure of the solo. Rhythm, dynamics, and range expand throughout the piece. Toots uses similar (measures five and nine) and contrasting (measures eight and eleven) elements for balance. The piece begins as it ends, on an upbeat D. Short and very tidy.

Toots is a pioneer and a great harp player. Without him, there would be very little jazz harp at all. See the discography at the end of this book for more titles featuring the master.

What Becomes of Your Life

Kal David and Harvey Brooks

Supplementary Discography

Captured Alive (Choice CRS 1007)
  Probably Toots's best small-group album.
Toots (Command RS930D)
  Not bad, but the accompaniment sounds a little square.
Yesterday and Today with Sven Asmussen (A&M 3613)
  Very nice.
Oscar Peterson's Big 6 at Montreaux (Pablo 2310747)
  Toots jams with a great rhythm section, and it's heavy.
Walking in Space – Quincy Jones (A&M SP3023)
  A great ballad, "I Never Told You," features Toots.
You Got It Bad, Girl – Quincy Jones (A&M 3613)
  One of Toots's favorites.

Cool Time

Miles Davis: So What

Miles Davis's album *Kind of Blue* was released in 1956. The album's cool, subtle tone was an unusual contrast to the then-popular hard bop style, which mixed the harmonic innovations of Charlie Parker with earthier, blues-based progressions. The tunes Davis created were beautifully simple: "So What" uses only two different chords in thirty-two bars, played at a gentle stroll. This in an era when players were jamming two, three, or four chord changes into every bar, at tempos that stopped just short of the speed of light!

Davis's solo on "So What" shows off many of the harmonic and rhythmic concepts of modern jazz in a context that's easier for the beginner to understand than most bebop. In addition, the tune is not a real chop-buster on the harp. All these things make it a good study for young jazz harp players.

Analysis

The chordal structure of the tune is simple: sixteen bars of D Minor, followed by eight bars of E♭ Minor, ending with another eight bars of D Minor. Davis's choice of notes is based almost entirely on the Dorian mode of each chord. Modes are different ways of ordering the notes of a scale. There are seven different modes, based on the seven different notes of the major scale. In the Dorian mode, the notes are arranged so that the major scale starts on its second degree. If we base the Dorian mode on D and E♭, respectively, and move up by thirds, we get the following:

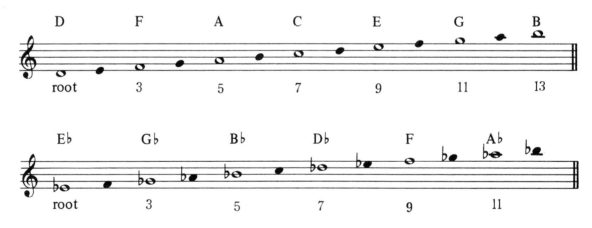

The triads formed by this progression of thirds are the basis for Davis's solo. In his first chorus, he uses the triad D-F-A over most of the D minor passages, with occasional nods to the "extension triad" C-E-G. In his second chorus, the D minor passages are pretty evenly divided up between D-F-A and C-E-G; the first eight bars work off the extension triad, the next eight bars off the tonic triad, and the last eight start with the extension and end solidly on the tonic. Listen to the solo so that you'll be able to connect this discussion with the sounds Davis puts down.

The E♭ minor bridge relies, in both choruses, on the D♭-F-A♭ extension. In fact, most of the time those passages sound as though they're in D♭ major rather than E♭ minor. This constant use of the extension notes, which are subtly dissonant, adds a lot of tension to what are really pretty bland chords.

Davis's rhythm is relaxed, but very unpredictable. Check out the startling end of the first phrase on the last beat of bar seven, the odd silence of bar twelve, the accent on the weak second beat of measure fourteen, the ear-catching placement of the F in bar thirty, etc. When the chord changes of a tune don't move much, rhythm becomes that much more important, so check out Davis's timing carefully.

Harp How-To

Because the tune is very easy to play on the chrom, but only parts of it fit the Marine Band, there's no blues harp notation included here. If you want to experiment, the D minor sections aren't too bad on the C harp, 3rd position. The E♭ minor sections can barely be played with overblows, or by switching harps.

On the chrom, pay attention to Davis's pitch shadings, such as on the high A♭ in bar twenty-three, and match them with a bend when possible. Try for the same feeling of power in reserve that Davis has. Play smooth and legato—connect your notes.

Oh, yes—we're going to work this out in all twelve keys, right? You betcha!

Chromatic pattern—minor 3rds

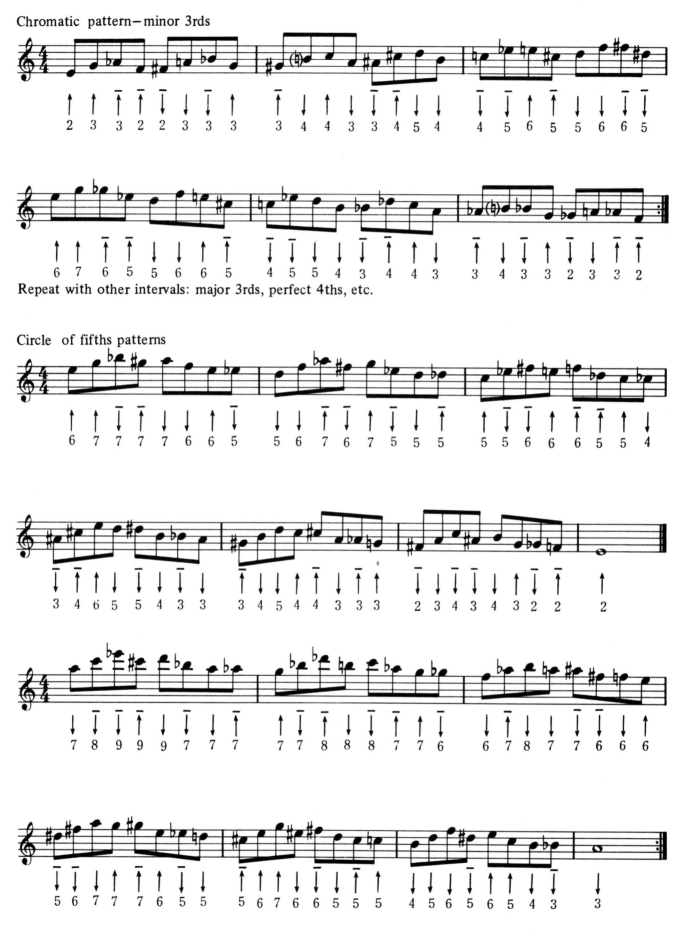

Repeat with other intervals: major 3rds, perfect 4ths, etc.

Circle of fifths patterns

30

So What

Miles Davis

Supplementary Discography

My Funny Valentine (Columbia PC-9106)
A concert recording of one of Miles's great bands on a great night.

Birth of the Cool (Capitol M-11026)
A landmark session. Small orchestra; relaxed, swinging music.

In a Silent Way (Columbia PC-9875)
Ditto.

Bitches Brew (Columbia PG-26)
Ditto ditto. This album and the preceding one had a lot to do with bringing elements of rock into the jazz mainstream.

My Favorite Things	John Coltrane Quartet	(Atlantic 1361)
Giant Steps	John Coltrane Quartet	(Atlantic 1311)
A Love Supreme	John Coltrane Quartet	(Impulse 77)
Ascension	John Coltrane	(Impulse 95)

These four albums, representative of Coltrane's various styles, are required listening for anyone who wants to know what the most recent peak in jazz saxophone technique and conception, not to mention composition, sounded like.

The Greatest Jazz Concert Ever (Prestige 24024)
It might be true. It's certainly a great set. Charlie Parker, Dizzy Gillespie, Bud Powell, Charlie Mingus, and Max Roach. Every one of these men was a virtuoso player, all were good composers and fine bandleaders. They play the hell out of the music, which is bebop, of course.

You Don't Have to Be a Star, Baby

Mike Turk: Old Man Adams

Mike Turk has been well known in the Boston area for years, but is unknown in most of the rest of the country. (Why is it that so many great harp players are unknown outside of their own backyards? So many hot players are rumors and legends. I've heard of a guy in D.C. who files the reeds on a Marine Band to make special tunings that he uses to play bebop; I've met Victor Pankow, the Brooklyn player who, among other things, is supposed to have invented alternate-side-of-the-mouth tongue blocking in 1914; I've heard of Noah Lewis, the blues harp player who supposedly led a big swing band, unamplified and loud as hell; but I've never heard a note from any of them. Why aren't they on prime-time TV? Let's all write to the networks and propose a weekly "Boss Harp" hour. First show: a Little Walter retrospective.)

Anyway, Mike Turk. Although Mike says that he had just begun serious study of the chromatic when he recorded this piece, his ideas and delivery are as polished as can be. He has a strong tone, with a gutsy vibrato, and his bending is blue and powerful—especially in the low-end passages at the beginning of the fourth chorus.

This transcription isn't a solo break; Turk's harp accompanies the vocal. Too many harp players don't seem to be able to accompany a singer without taking over the tune. Turk's playing here actually lights up the lyrics, sensitively but with plenty of power. Listen carefully to the record for insight into how Turk lets the lyrics guide him through this piece.

Analysis

The tune is made up of a verse in D major and a chorus in B minor. This is very simple stuff, so Turk shows only a few flashes of virtuosity. His approach is to concentrate on developing a few melodic and rhythmic ideas, every now and then throwing in a hot lick to keep you listening, and finishing up with the hottest lick of all.

On the first chorus, Turk establishes the main melodic element—B rising E, then up or down to A—and the rhythmic motif of a dotted half note (three beats) followed by some division of a quarter note (one beat):

The second chorus doubles up the phrasing of the first,

and adds the first hot run—a two-octave glide the entire range of the solo, from high to low A. The repeated lick that follows the run,

has a bluesy feel because of the C natural (flat 7th of D).

In the third verse, Turk begins to wail. Notice how long he's held back before getting heavy. It's almost like a duet between harp and voice here. Notice how Turk climbs to the bright E when the lyric comes to the word "high." The last chorus reverses the B to E motion of the others,

and ends with another two-octave run.

The last repeat of the chorus is real blue and moaning. Topping it all off is a nice guitar and harp lick, and a great little harp cadenza. Again, see how Turk saves the best for last.

Harp How-To

Because this is just about as easy (or hard) on the C chrom as on the G chrom that Turk used, I've notated the transcription for both. The fast run at the end sounds harder to play than it is. A lot of the motion is simple slide work. Practice *slowly* and don't take it up to tempo until you know the notes well. Be clean!

Turk's bending gives the chrom a wailing sound that I like. You can read a bit about bending the chrom in the chapters on Stevie Wonder and Toots Thielemans—now listen to how Turk uses his bends to make the lyrics work. Turk's throat vibrato is also important in giving his lines a haunting, lyrical feel.

Watch out for Turk—and your own local hotshots—wherever you might find them. Remember, musicians with double platinum records aren't the only ones who have a lot to say.

Old Man Adams

Richard Johnson

Swing Harp Roots

The Harmonicats: Harmonica Boogie

The Harmonicats are probably the most famous of all harmonica trios (the usual trio has bass, 48 chord-rhythm, and chromatic harps). Their recording of "Peg O' My Heart" sold 10 million copies, and that ain't hay. They were very good players, with plenty of chops and lots of ideas.

This solo is one of the very best first-position Marine Band solos ever recorded. The style is completely different from the high register stuff you'd hear out of Jimmy Reed or Walter Horton; learning this one will really improve your ability to move around the top end of the harp. Don't ignore the chorded chrom solo or the 48-chord rhythm harp solo on this record either!

Analysis

The solo goes for four choruses of a twelve-bar blues. The tone is very clear, almost flute-like, without a trace of vibrato. The piece is played way high up, never going below blow 5 on the Marine Band, so that the bending all takes place on the blow 8, 9, and 10 reeds. In first position in the top octave, you can only get the flat 7th (C natural in the key of D) by bending blow 10, which doesn't happen here, so the natural 7th (C♯) is used throughout. That's not necessarily bad—Charlie Parker usually stuck to the natural 7th on the first three bars of a twelve-bar—but it does take some of the blue out of the piece. On a light-hearted tune like this, nasty blue notes aren't too badly missed.

The first eight bars of the first chorus are built on the fifth of the scale, with melodic and rhythmic variations on the opening riff. There is a lot of motion, mostly scalar, in measure nine, with a fair amount of the over-and-under approach to chord tones that jazz players use, in bars ten-eleven. Dig the little shakes, almost grace notes, that pop up here and there. This trick is easy, and is sort of equivalent to the shakes and turns that chromatic players work with the slide.

In the second chorus, there's a lot of motion, again mostly scalar, or by thirds (adjacent blow or draw notes). I don't think these lines should be engraved on stone tablets, but the guy sure knows his way around the top end of the Marine Band.

The bends in this solo are all short, and quickly resolve upwards. There's a lot more you can do with those upper register bends—check out Wonder's "Boogie On Reggae Woman," or Jimmy Reed—but the light bends suit this piece well. They sound pretty hip in the third chorus, with that repeated lick on blow 9 to 10.

Harp How-To

This piece requires fast, accurate breathing. (Better lay off the tobacco, pal.) The best way to get that is to practise *slowly,* bringing out the quick stuff when you know where you're going. Try to get the same clear, beautiful tone that you hear on the record. Breathe evenly from your gut, and leave your mean vibrato at home.

I have a lot of affection for this piece. You can tell that the Harmonicats had a lot of fun doing it. Supplement what you learn from this tune with some listening to John Lee (Sonny Boy I) Williamson, Jimmy Reed, and Walter Horton, and you'll have yourself some dandy first-position chops. Check out the Marine Band exercises on scales and alternating thirds for some practise on the techniques you'll need for this number.

Harmonica Boogie

Jerry Murad

Marine Band in D

(actual pitch: octave higher)

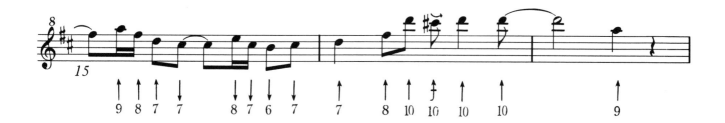

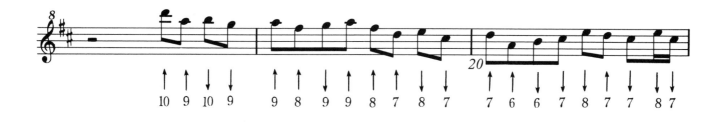

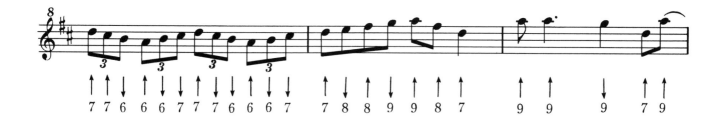

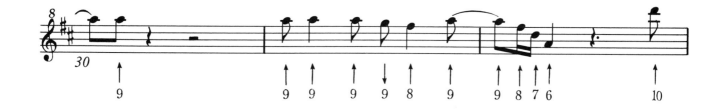

43

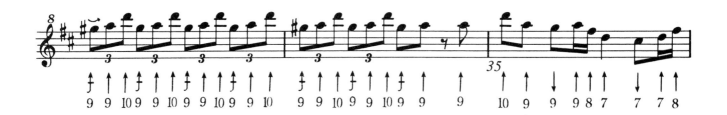

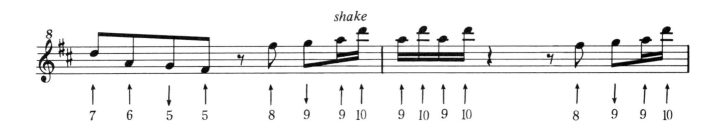

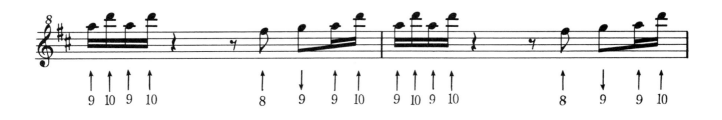

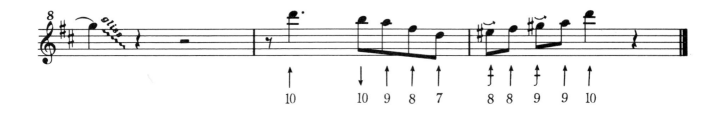

44

Blue Saxophone

King Curtis: Honky Tonk

King Curtis was one of the best R&B tenor saxophonists who ever lived, and a very good hard bop player before that. His work has been imitated at one time or another by just about every R&B saxophonist. He was killed at the age of forty-one by a junkie who was shooting up on the steps of Curtis's apartment house. If anyone ever offers you heroin, my friends, I hope you will remember that too many good people have already died from that poison, including many great musicians.

This solo is easy to analyze, and contains all sorts of different intervals, rhythms, and sounds. It's a great way for a harp player to see *exactly* how a horn player's approach to a simple blues differs from a blues harpist's.

Analysis

"Honky Tonk" is a twelve-bar blues, so the structure of the tune is familiar. The most important thing about the solo is Curtis's constant reworking of his tone, attack, and rhythmic approach. For example, the little riff that makes up the melody is changed at each appearance in the first eight bars of the tune—pitches are flatted, the rhythm is changed from triple to duple (along with momentary hints of double-time), tonguing changes from legato to staccato. Every aspect of Curtis's sound is flexible and alive. Listen to the recording with the transcription in front of you to check out the details of Curtis's interpretation.

A few other aspect of Curtis's style deserve mention here. First, his use of the high register is powerful and unique. He does not use runs leading into the high register, but hits a high note—usually the tonic—after a rest, and then quickly runs down to the midrange. In other words, he uses the high register for another kind of accent, as in these examples:

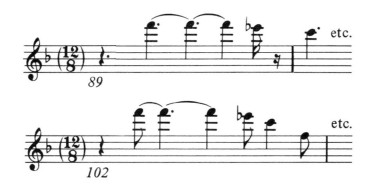

45

Second, he almost never uses the flat seventh (E♭ in the key of F) for anything but a descending run; he uses the sixth degree of the scale (D) when he wants to circle the tonic:

Remember that Curtis is allowed a lot of freedom in his tone because he's the soloist. Don't fool around like that when you're playing in a horn section—it will sound sloppy. Listen to Curtis's even attack when he plays the ensemble riff after his first solo.

Harp How-To

This solo is fairly tough to play on the harp, and I've had to do a lot of transposing, especially for the Marine Band. I've brought the chromatic up an octave from where Curtis played it, because I think it sounds better in that range, and because it can then be played on a three-octave chrom. Try it at the tenor's pitch—just subtract four from every chrom hole number—and see if you agree.

On the Marine Band, I had to break up some lines by transposing notes up or down an octave, and even changing a few pitches. Even so, the flavor of the lines is very nice. I've included some alternate hole numbers so you can try transposed lines in both octaves.

Practise the jumps—there are plenty—slowly, until you can hit them in your sleep. Stuff like this is never easy on the harp, but practise will make you more comfortable with jumps and sudden changes of direction. See the bending exercises below for help in learning to jump to and from a bend.

It's hard to get as flexible a tone on the harp as Curtis gets on the tenor sax, but if you listen carefully, the meaning of his tone and attack changes will come thorugh. By "meaning," I mean the precise way that sounds are shaped into phrases. Try to play his rhythms exactly; he tells his story in those sixteenth-note anticipations. You can imitate the growling sounds Curtis gets with a hard bend, using plenty of volume and perhaps a slight wah with the hand.

You're going to memorize this solo—or parts of it, anyway—in all 12 keys, aren't you? Enjoy yourself. Ya can't spell funk without fun.

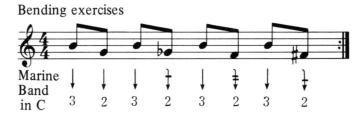

Bending exercises

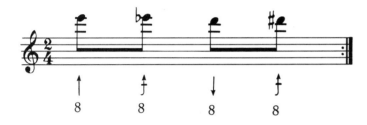

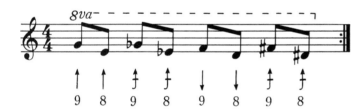

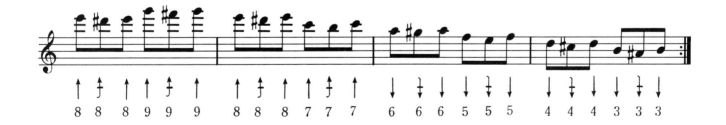

Honky Tonk

B. Doggett, S. Shephard, B. Butler, C. Scott

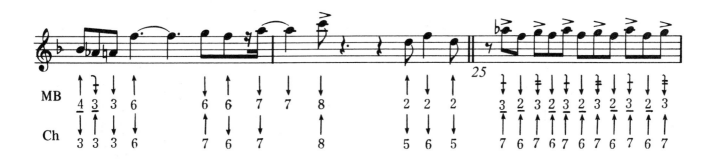

49

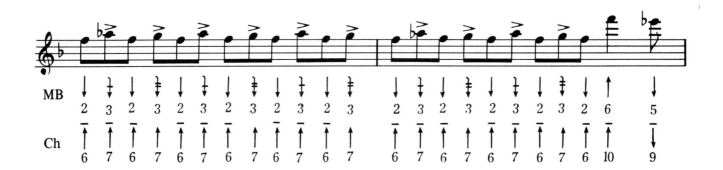

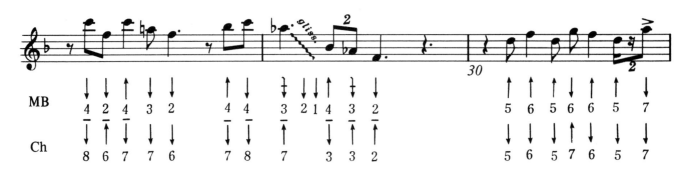

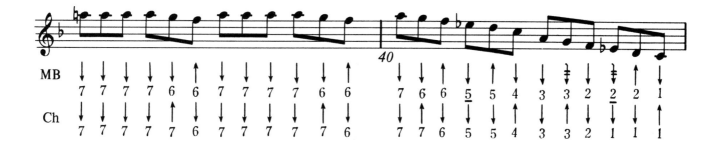

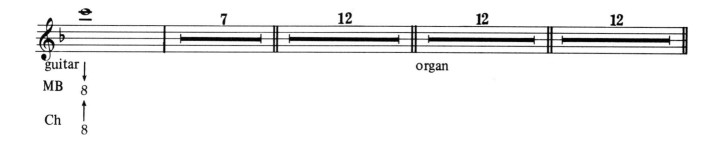

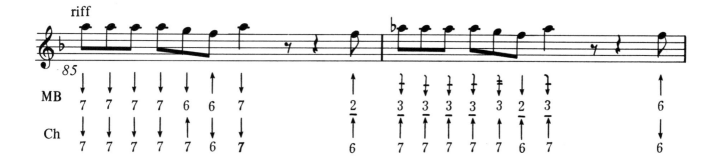

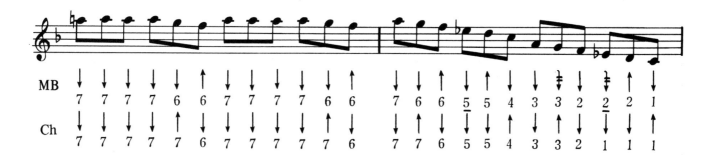

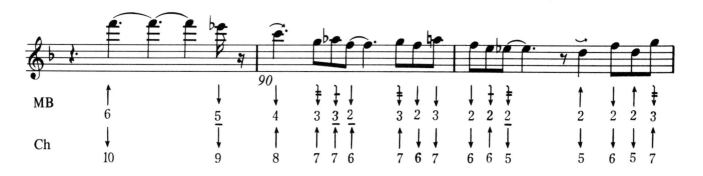

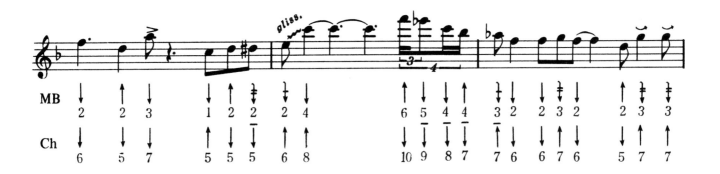

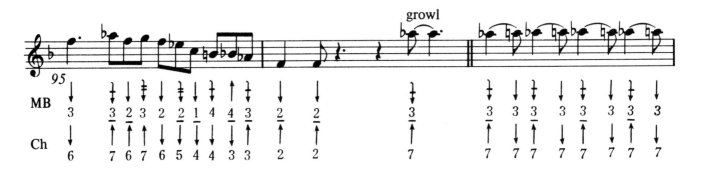

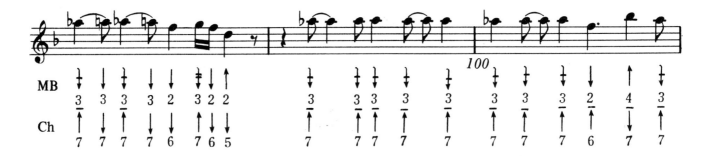

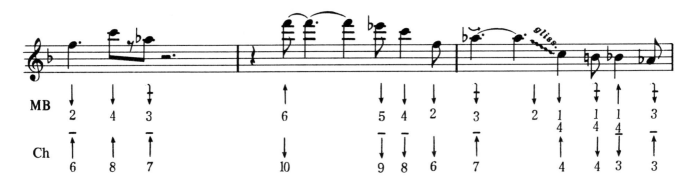

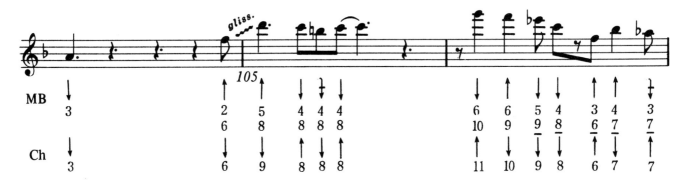

Supplementary Discography

Blues At Montreaux King Curtis with Champion Jack Dupree (Atlantic 1637)
King Curtis Live At The Fillmore West (Atco 33-359)

    Curtis plays all sorts of material here. It's rare to find someone who can cook so hard and play a melody so beautifully. Curtis's recording of "Memphis Soul Stew," which is a classic example of all-out R&B sax, should be available from singles and oldies dealers.

Rocking Sax

King Curtis: Ridin' Thumb

"Ridin' Thumb" makes a good companion to "Honky Tonk." Although the melodic vocabularies are similar, "Honky Tonk" is relaxed, while "Ridin' Thumb" is driving. This difference is partly due to the phrasing, which is longer and more regular on "Honky Tonk." Curtis uses four-bar phrases on the blues, integrated into the twelve-bar pattern. He uses irregular-length phrases and long rests between phrases to produce flurries of motion, especially in his second solo on "Ridin' Thumb." Notice the three-measure long blast on the fifth of the scale that starts the last phrase in the second solo. The effect is climactic, just as it is in Louis Armstrong's "West End Blues."

Curtis's tone on "Ridin' Thumb" is harder and rougher than on "Honky Tonk," with fewer contrasts. A quiet, thoughtful solo here wouldn't cut through the band in full cry. Many amplified harp players tend to rely on certain notes for the same reason: No matter how hard you're playing, you can always get some articulation out of the low- and mid-range draw reeds and high-range blow reeds on a Marine Band.

Notice that here, as in "Honky Tonk," Curtis resolves the flat seventh of the scale (B natural in the key of D♭) downward:

Except for the occasional flat seventh, Curtis sticks pretty close to the notes of the pentatonic scale.

D♭ pentatonic scale

An exception to this is the last phrase in the second solo;

which is built on a D♭ blues scale. This last blue phrase is a nice contrast to all the pentatonic lines, and really seals the ending.

Harp How-To

The piece sounds good on both chromatic and Marine Band. D♮ is not a bad key for the chrom—much of the piece can be played with the slide held in. On the Marine Band, only a couple of notes have to be transposed. The eleventh measure of the first solo may give you a little trouble:

You'll need to practise the fast jump up and down a fifth in order to get the proper punch into the low note. This lick is much easier, one octave higher on the blues harp (blow 6, draw 6, draw 4, draw 6, blow 6).

Practise the downward bluesy run that ends the second solo slowly before you take it up to tempo. You can get a mild but effective bend on the upper register draw reeds of the Marine Band that'll serve as an imitation of the winding bend that Curtis uses on the high A♭. None of the other runs or jumps are very hard. If you use a pucker, tonguing lightly before or after a jump may make it easier to avoid the notes between. Don't tongue too hard or you'll interrupt the flow of the lines.

This is a very good piece to work out in all twelve keys on the chromatic, since the material is classic R&B. It's also a thoughtful piece, full of surprising touches. (Yes, you can be thoughtful even while you're blowing your brains out, and the best always are.) For example, the first and second phrases in the second solo, which are irregular in length, are nevertheless balanced: Each ends on a dissonance a fifth below its starting note, with nearly identical rhythms in the last measure, followed by a long rest.

Curtis's sense of rightness, his ability to avoid cliches and overstatement in a style that leans to both, is something special.

Transposing

Transposing isn't hard, but until you know your scales well it will take time. The more you do it, the quicker you'll be, so let's get down to it.

One fairly simple way to transpose is to number the notes of a passage according to their scale position in the original key, then find the notes that match those positions in the new key. For example, King Curtis's "Ridin' Thumb" in Db :

and in A:

Another way is to find the interval between the original key and the new one, and shift all the notes up or down by that interval.

Let's take the beginning of "So What." The original is in D minor. To transpose it into Bb minor, first find the interval between D and Bb —down a major 3rd. Then, move every note down a major 3rd. Starting with:

A major 3rd below D is Bb, below C is Ab, below F is Db , below A is F, etc. So you wind up with:

Once you really know your scales—by ear as well as by rote— you can just wing it and let your ears guide you. In the meantime, try both methods, and see which works better for you.

Pentatonic runs (flat third for minor)

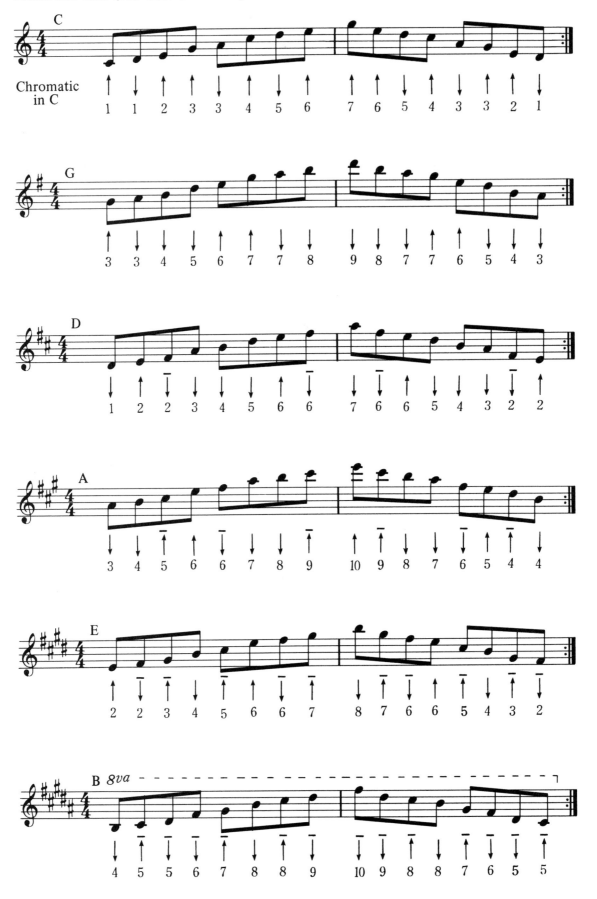

Chromatic in C

58

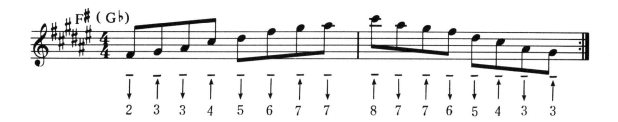

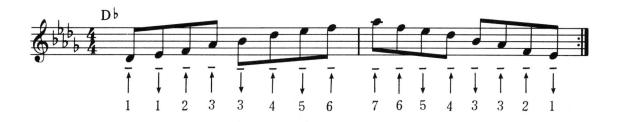

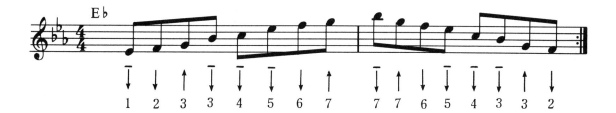

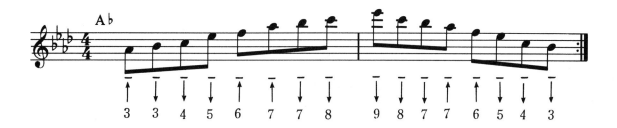

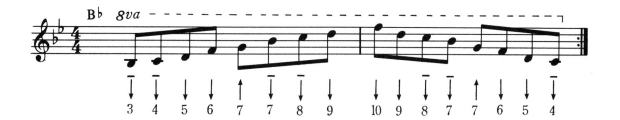

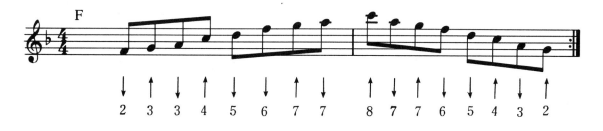

Pentatonic runs

Marine Band in C

(second position)

(second position)

(first position)

(first position)

(sixth position)

60

Ridin' Thumb

James Seals and Dash Crofts

*The intro may be played as follows to simulate more closely Curtis's attack.

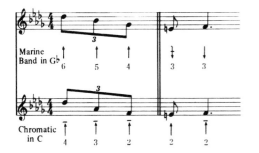

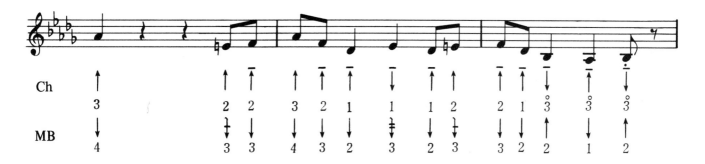

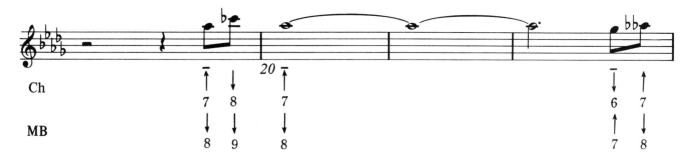

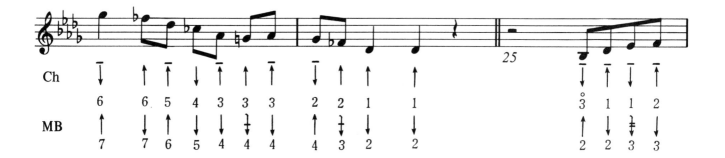

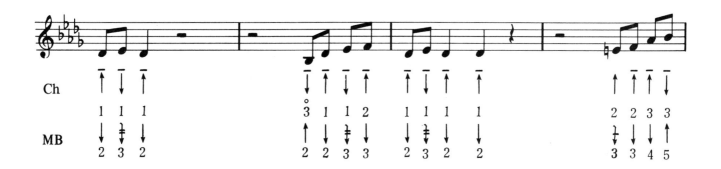

The Hottest R&B Harp

Stevie Wonder: For Once in My Life; Creepin'; Please Don't Go

Stevie Wonder is probably the most popular harp player in the world, and one of the best. His style leans more towards R&B than jazz, but he can make nice melodies on all sorts of material, and he swings hard.

Wonder uses a certain few techniques in almost everything he does. Almost all his recordings have one or more passages in which Wonder trills or makes a turn with the slide. "I Was Made To Love Her" has a good example in the intro:

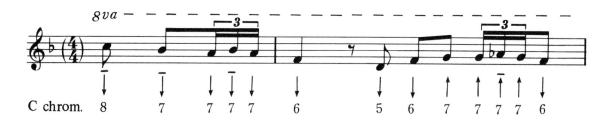

Wonder uses this trick in different keys: "Fingertips" is in D minor, "I Was Made to Love Her" is in F, "Please Don't Go" is in G, etc. This is also in Toots Thielemans's bag of tricks. See "What Becomes Of Your Life" in this book, and dig this phrase from Toots's solo on "Snooze," from the *Captured Alive* LP:

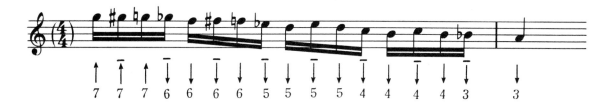

Wonder's attack is usually marcato (slightly separated) rather than legato. His notes sometimes have a ragged edge to their tails, which gives them an urgent sound. He tongues fairly hard, especially on repeated notes. He often uses repeated notes to get the rhythm cooking:

from "For Once in My Life":

from "Creepin' ":

Like Toots, he doesn't use much vibrato, and he rarely if ever uses his hands to shape his tone.

Many of his solos, like those of King Curtis, are built mainly on the pentatonic scale. This type of scale is very easy in the key of F♯ (G♭) on the chrom, and can also be played very loudly in that key. Both "Creepin' " and "For Once in My Life" are in F♯. Wonder has a different approach to the high register from Curtis. Curtis hits a blast in the stratosphere without warning and comes down right away, while Wonder usually builds up carefully to a high end climax in his solos. All of the solos in this chapter work that way—the last screaming A♯ in "For Once in My Life" is a real ripper.

These solos, for all that they sound amazing, aren't very hard to play once you can get a strong, clean tone out of the chromatic. Of course there are a few little nasty parts. One of those is the bend that begins "Please Don't Go." Folks who haven't done much bending on the chrom will probably have some trouble getting a B♭ to bend down below an A, but it's not impossible. Any technique that gives a good bend on the blues harp will work on the chrom, but don't hit the reed too hard or the note will blank out or jump to a high harmonic. (Don't feel too bad. Even Toots does it once on the Montreux jam album.)

"Creepin' " also starts with a hard bend, but this should be a little easier, since he works it in after he's started the note.

The fifth measure of "For Once in My Life" has a fast jump from D♯ to G that may be troublesome:

Practise some extension exercises, and don't play it at tempo until you can play it clean.

These solos, along with King Curtis's, will show you a few of the things that you can do with pentatonic scales. Pentatonic scales for Marine Band and chrom are listed at the end of the sections on Curtis. Check it out.

Stevie Wonder, along with Toots Thielemans, *is* modern jazz harp. Don't pass him by.

For Once in My Life

Orlando Murden and Ronald Miller

Chromatic in C

Creepin'

Stevie Wonder

Chromatic in C

Please Don't Go

Stevie Wonder

Chromatic in C

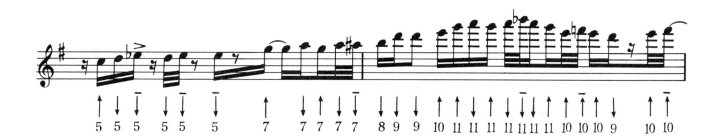

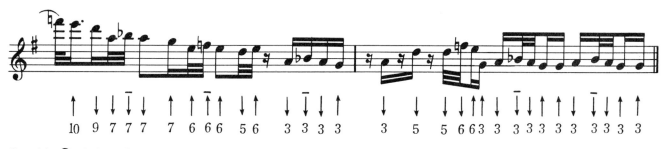

Supplementary Discography

Fingertips parts I & II   Stevie Wonder   (Motown 407)
We Can Work It Out   Stevie Wonder   (Motown 530)
I Was Made to Love Her Steve Wonder   (Motown 418)

These were all released as singles, and all have great harp. Dealers in singles and oldies will have them.

Innervisions   Stevie Wonder   (Tamla 7-326L)
Songs in the Key of Life Stevie Wonder   (Tamla 13-34002)

These albums have fine harp work, and the best American popular music since Gershwin. I've also heard of, but never seen, an album titled *Eivets Rednow,* which has excellent versions of standards like "Alfie" by Eivets himself.

The First Great Jazz Soloist

Louis Armstrong: West End Blues

Many people have written about "West End Blues," and most say that it's a masterpiece; maybe one of the greatest in jazz. The solo will show you a way to play the blues that most harp players never come close to, not because it's that hard technically but because the thinking involved is so different from blues harp. Blues harp players usually build a twelve-bar chorus from a series of riffs as Little Walter does. Walter almost always repeats one- or two-bar riffs to make up his larger phrases, changing riffs as the chords move. Armstrong, on the other hand, plays lines that get longer and longer, with little or no outright repetition.

I don't think there's any doubt that Armstrong *is* jazz, while Walter is jazz-influenced. In other words, a perfect understanding of Walter (and all the other great blues players) is not enough to play jazz, or even a jazz blues. Let's get particular with this solo, and see why.

Analysis

First notice the shapes of Armstrong's lines. In measure eight of the intro, Armstrong zeroes in on an F minor chord (II of E♭):

See how he circles around it, hitting, in order, the 5th, root, and 3rd of the chord (C,F, A♭); approaching the tonic from below and above (E,G); then sounding the tonic, 5th, and 7th of the chord (F, C, E♭), which itself is an over-and-under approach to the 3rd of the next chord (B♭⁷). The same kind of approach to the notes of a target chord can be seen in these two excerpts from Armstrong's first chorus.

In general, Armstrong uses strong chord tones as his goals, moving around to attack them from both directions, usually by stepwise motion.

Take another look at the cadence above from measures nine-ten. Compare that line to these cadences from a later Armstrong blues:

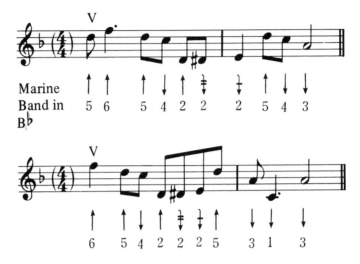

In each case, Armstrong rises chromatically from the 9th of the V^7 chord to the 3rd, jumps up a sixth or a seventh, then drops down to the 13th of the V^7 chord (the 3rd of the tonic chord that follows). If you play through these examples you'll hear how nice that particular sequence of notes is. In second position on a blues harp, these lines are not hard to play once you get the jumps down.

Throughout the solo, Armstrong leans heavily on the fifth of the E♭ scale (B♭). The first chorus begins with a long B♭, and the first phrase ends on a long B♭ an octave lower. The IV chord arrives and leaves on the same note, and the first chorus ends on a long, high B♭. Armstrong's second chorus begins with a powerful four-measure long B♭, then hits it four times in a repeated lick that harks back to bar five of the intro. The fifth is the most stable note of the scale after the tonic, and Little Walter and King Curtis, among others, often put a lot of power behind it in their solos. Check out "Ridin' Thumb" in this book, and dig Walter's "Off The Wall."

Harp How-To

Although this piece isn't very hard on the harp, certain notes can't be played on the Marine Band. Again, I've substituted notes that I think preserve the shape and feel of the lines. The D in bar seventeen has been transposed down an octave although you could also play it with an overblow on blow 5. The low G in bar sixteen has been changed to an A♭. If you disagree with my choices, you can make your own, or stick to the chromatic.

There are a lot of jumps in this piece. Good tongue blockers can handle it without much trouble. People who pucker should concentrate on moving the harp in an arc, rather than straight across the mouth, and tongue lightly if necessary before or after a jump to keep the inner notes from playing. Practise slowly until you have control.

Listen carefully to this and all the other tunes on the Armstrong and Hines LP. Music is *sound*; don't rely solely on a transcription to show you what's happening. What transcription could convey such a classic piece of Armstrong as the way he does a glissando from the bottom to the top of the horn, bringing up the volume until the last note blasts out like a freight train? Jazz, man.

West End Blues

Clarence Williams and Joe Oliver

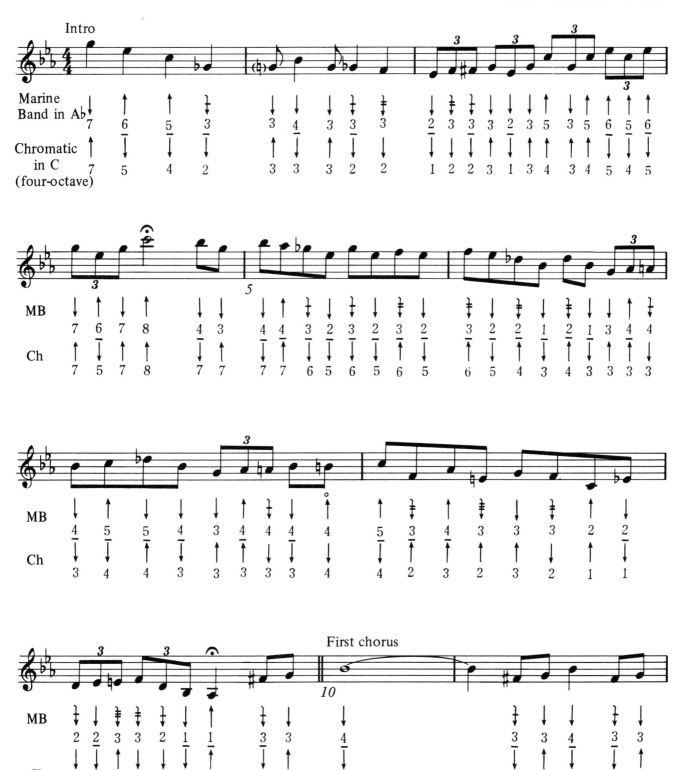

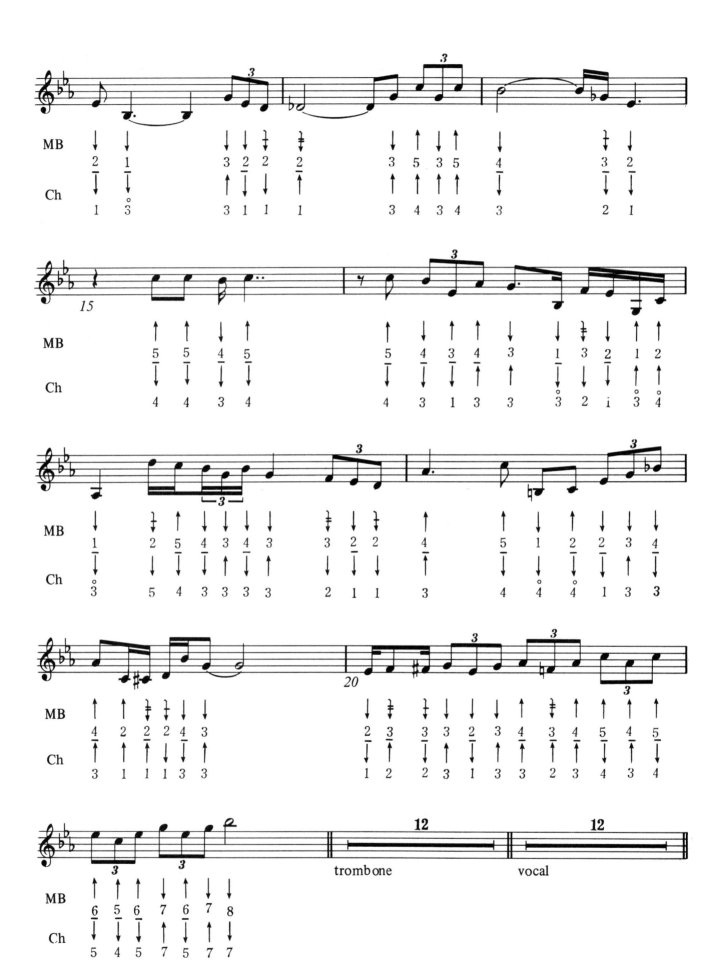

74

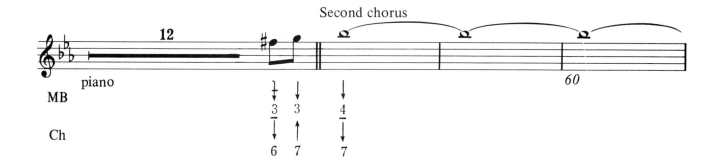

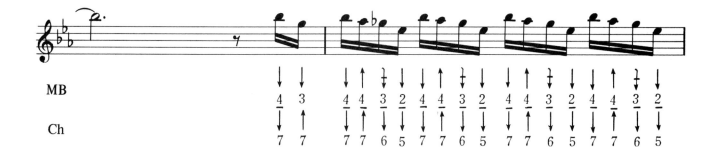

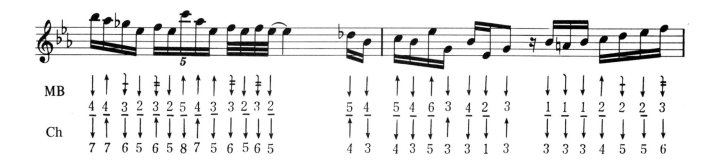

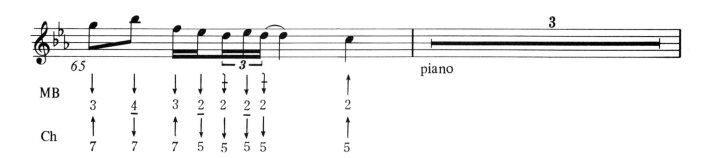

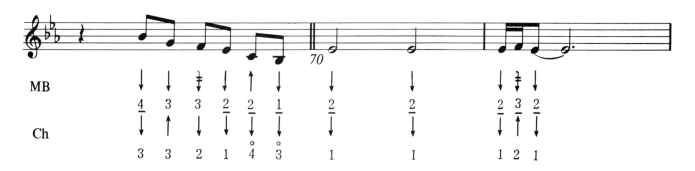

Supplementary Discography

Louis Armstrong: An Early Portrait (Milestone MLP-2010)
   Armstrong with Ma Rainey, Fletcher Henderson, and others.
Sidney Bechet: Superb Sidney (French CBS mono 62636)
   Bechet worked with Armstrong on many occasions. His clarinet and soprano sax work here
   shows a very bravura approach to early jazz.
The Commodore Years — The Tenor Sax: Lester Young, Chu Berry, and Ben Webster
(Atlantic SD2-307)
   These sides show the later development of Armstrong's innovations by three top tenor
   players just prior to the bebop era.
In a Mellotone   Duke Ellington Orchestra (RCA LPM-1364)
At His Very Best   Duke Ellington Orchestra (RCA LPM-17175)
   These albums show off the 1939-41 Ellington band, one of the greatest of all jazz big
   bands. The solos are very much in the Armstrong mold, and the arrangements are classic.

A New Style in Marine Band Solo

Richard Hunter: Winter Sun at Nobska

My stuff! Hot ziggety. This is the only piece in this book written specifically for harp without accompaniment, and I'm sure you've never heard anything like it. There are no bends or chords, and the piece doesn't go below the second octave of the Marine Band. The structure of the piece is more out of modern jazz than the blues, with hints of Bartók and Debussy.

"Winter Sun" will have you solving problems of tone control and breathing in a context very different from boogie music, and will show you some things about unaccompanied harp that you'll never learn from playing a train. Real solo harp is almost a forgotten art nowadays. Check out Larry Adler's "Malaqueña" if you can find it; I guarantee it'll open your eyes.

The piece is notated for an F harp, though I often play it on an E harp. In any case, you won't get the right tone on anything lower than a D. I like the sound of wood for this number, so I usually use an Orchestre. A Golden Melody that's perfectly in tune is fine too. (Mels sound worse than anything when they're out of tune.)

Analysis

The piece is built on two Minor 7th chord arpeggios, the second an extension of the first. Climaxes are on the note midway between the farthest points:

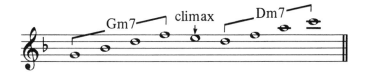

The first arpeggio is played in triplets going up and then down; the second down and then up. The arpeggios should be played fast and clear, with a slight accent on the first note of each triplet. Play softly—this is background material—and swell the arpeggio slightly as you go up, so that it peaks just as you change direction. At the climaxes on draw 7, start the note quietly and then bring up the volume. *Don't* use a throat vibrato. The breathing exercises at the end of the book will help you keep an even tone, and the extension exercises will help you with the two jumps of a 5th that lead down to the first draw 7:

The interlude after the fermata () in measure twenty-eight:

should be gradually speeded up until you're racing around blow 8. Put a lot of force into the draw 7 that follows. The return of the arpeggio should swell and then fade to nothing. When the high arpeggio begins, bring it in at a whisper and then raise the volume, to make it sound like it's approaching from a distance. The last section:

should accelerate until the drop to draw 6, followed by the long cry on draw 7, that makes the final climax.

The last run, with all the notes of both arpeggios,

should be played fast, with rising volume, and a quick, clean rush of air on the blow 9 that ends the piece.

The piece looks hard on paper, but the feeling isn't hard to understand. Listen to the recording, and use the notation as a guide once you have the music in your head.

The piece is improvisational in the sense that you can stretch out or condense any section in performance. Add your own ideas if you like, but remember that a simple piece won't carry a ton of freight.

Breathe long and slow on this piece. The fermatas are a good place to catch your breath, but don't be noisy; there's a lot of silence, here.

Imagine that you're a solitary bird whistling on a cold winter day. In the silence you hear the summer singing. You give a long low trill and a glad chirp and are suddenly still.

Winter Sun at Nobska

Richard Hunter

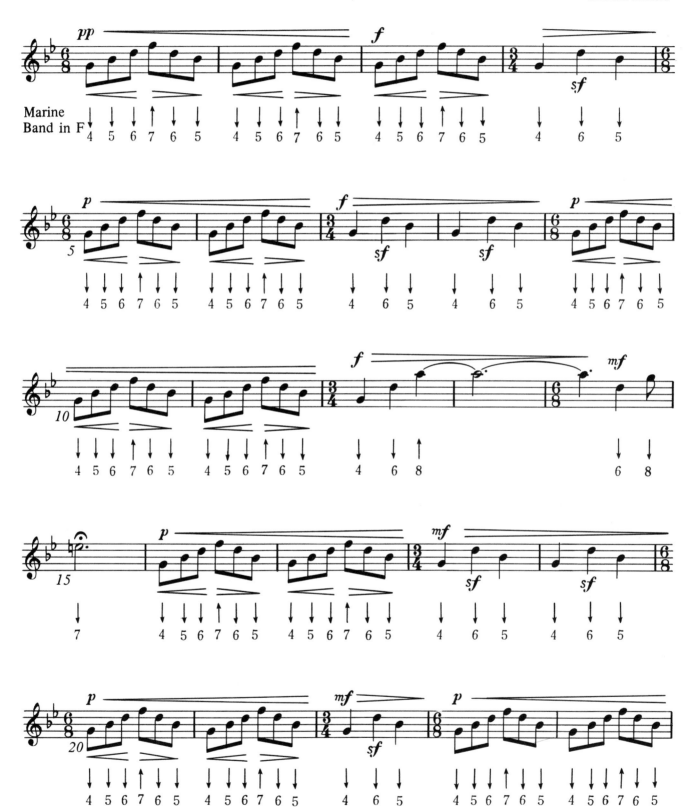

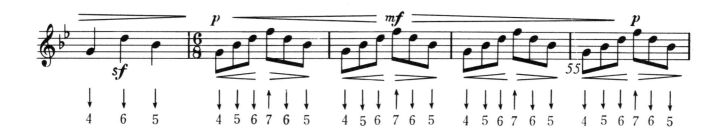

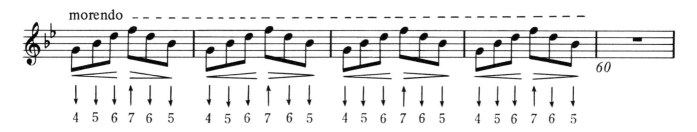

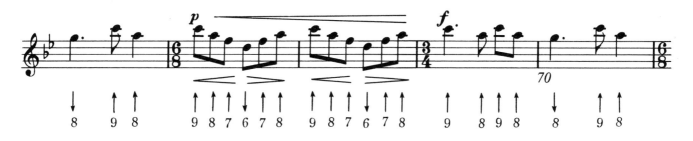

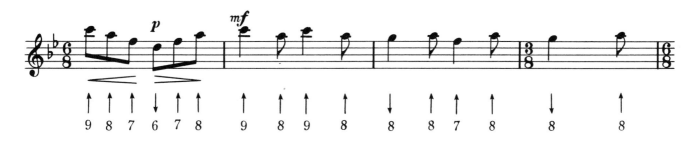

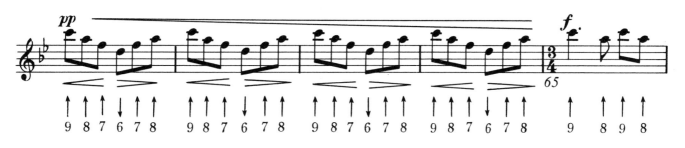

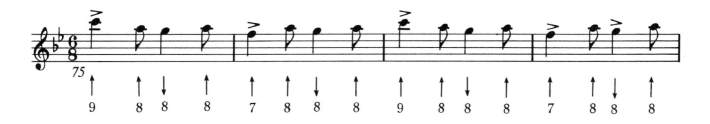

Supplementary Listening

Listen to music by Béla Bartók and Claude Debussy for examples of what the structure and harmony of my piece are severely reduced from. These composers both wrote extensively for solo piano, and their music is available on hundreds of different recordings. Check it out to see how a solo performance can be sustained over long periods of time, and dig the harmonies.

Great solo jazz performances have been recorded by Keith Jarrett, Bill Evans, Art Tatum, Cecil Taylor, Earl Hines, McCoy Tyner, and hundreds of others. These guys are all pianists, by the way—there aren't too many solo harp recordings available, except for trains and such. It's possible to learn something from these players about the structure of an extended jazz piece played solo even if you don't play the piano.

A Slightly
Pre-Bebop Blues

Charlie Christian:
Gone with What Wind

Charlie Christian, the first great jazz guitarist, was one of the people who contributed heavily to the creation of bebop. The techniques of harmonic and melodic construction that were developed in the bebop era are still powerful forces in modern jazz today. Christian had only reached his early twenties when he died in 1942, but the style he created has echoed in the work of almost every jazz guitarist since.

Christian had a lot of blues in his playing. This piece, which he recorded with the Benny Goodman Sextet, shows off his mixture of basic blues feeling and higher harmonic intervals, along with shapes and lines that will be new to but not too difficult for most harp players. This two-chorus solo is the take originally released, although the version on the Columbia LP *Solo Flight* contains additional solo choruses by Christian.

Analysis

The tune is a blues in C, so we should all be familiar with the structure. Christian, like Armstrong, used strong chord tones—root, 3rd, 5th, 7th, and 9th—as target notes, approaching them stepwise from above or below, or from both directions:

or just stringing them together in arpeggios. He liked to run two arpeggios together, the first going one way and the second running back the other way:

This gave him plenty of motion without dragging him all over the place, and kept the harmony clear. He used close intervals:

as contrast to the spread-out arpeggios.

Higher chord intervals are brought in gradually. The first 7th we see is in bar four, setting up the F^7 chord in bar five. The 9th of F appears briefly in bar six:

In this case he was probably thinking melodically rather than harmonically—the G is part of a push down to E (3rd of C). The run on a G^9 arpeggio that starts in bar twenty-one is a real earcatcher. He approached the 9th (A) from below (G♯), then gave us a G^9 arpeggio running down, up, then down again, with chromatic motion down to G in bar twenty-two and C in bar twenty-three anchoring the chord. Christian often used chromatic motion down to the root or 5th of a chord from a whole step above to emphasize these stable tones in a line.

Christian thought mostly in terms of arpeggios and bluesy riffs. This is common with swing players—check out Lester Young or Coleman Hawkins—but very few harp players think that way, probably because arpeggios often involve big jumps, making them tricky on the harp. But the nice sound makes it worth the trouble of learning a few things in that style. Check out the arpeggios for Marine Band and chrom at the end of the book, and practise, practise, practise!

Harp How-To

The solo isn't too hard to play on the chrom, but the second chorus will give Marine Band players a few headaches. The G^9 runs that start in measure twenty-one are just about impossible to play on the Marine Band: The notes aren't there. In order to make those lines fit, I've transposed them up an octave and changed some pitches:

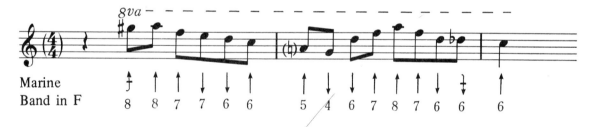

This saves the overall shape of the lines, and sounds similar, but anyone who wants to do it like Christian will have to do it on the chrom. The E♭ in bar twelve has been changed to E natural (draw 7), but you can play the E♭ with an overblow on blow 6. See the bending exercises in the chapters on Scott and Curtis for help in getting your bends more precise.

None of the jumps are real mind-bogglers. Remember to move the harp in an arc, rather than straight across your mouth. The sudden directional shifts that Christian used will be easier after practise.

An excellent jazz pianist once told me that he liked to check out guitar players because their lines are so different from those that come naturally to pianists. On the harp, that kind of thinking is even more important. Stravinsky once said, "Poor composers tend to borrow, and good composers tend to steal." Be a clever, open-minded theif.

Gone with What Wind

Benny Goodman and Count Basie

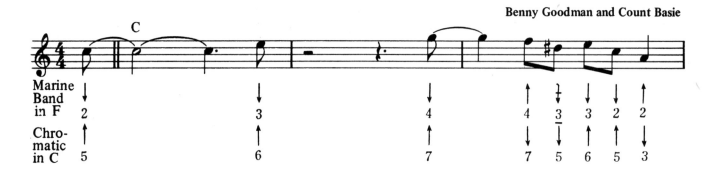

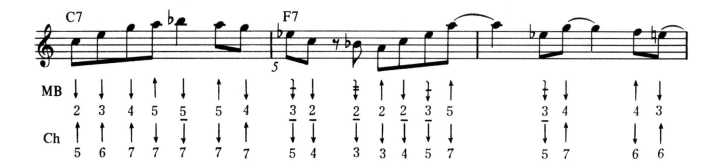

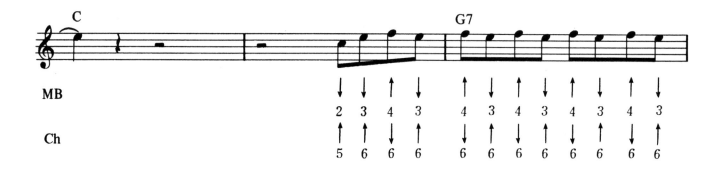

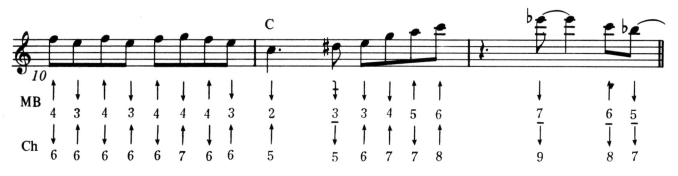

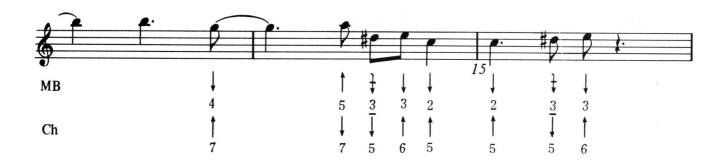

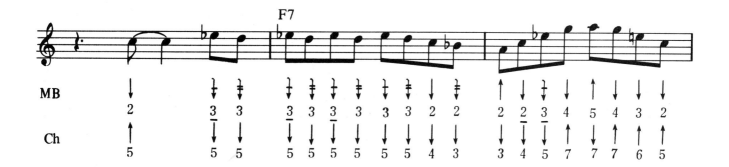

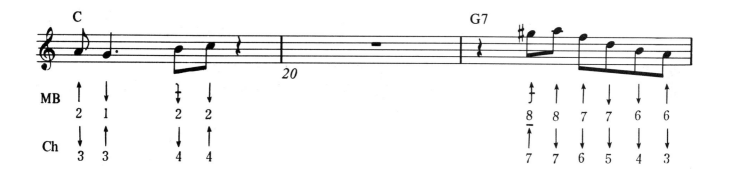

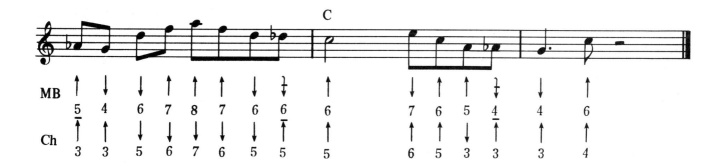

Supplementary Discography

From Spirituals to Swing (Vanguard VSD 47/48)
    This two-record set documents the 1938/39 "Spirituals to Swing" Carnegie Hall concerts. Great stuff by Christian, Goodman, Lester Young, Sonny Terry, the Golden Gate Quartet, and more.

Modern Harmonica Technique

There are two basic ways to get a single note out of a harp. You can *pucker*, or narrow your lips down until there's just enough space to let a single note play; or you can *tongue block*, covering several holes with your mouth while your tongue blocks off one or more reeds. (This won't be news to most people reading this book, but please bear with me. There are some very good players who don't know all the ins and outs of these two very different techniques.) Tongue blocking makes many things, like long jumps and all sorts of chording, much easier, but puckering has its advantages, too. It's my opinion that a really good player will know something about both styles, and use whichever one is best suited for the music at hand.

Basic Techniques and Their Application

For classical music, tongue blocking is the only way to go. Many passages from the music of Bach, for instance, feature lines that change direction almost constantly, often leaping a 4th or more in the process. You can't play a line like that legato with a pucker because when you shift the harp, you break the line, even if for only an instant. With a tongue block, by simply shifting your tongue from one side of the mouth to the other you can jump an octave or more with ease.

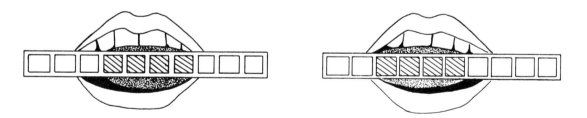

In the illustration, the mouth covers five holes—an octave on the chrom. When the tongue covers the four holes to the left, the high notes plays; shift the tongue to the right, and you get the low note.

Both tongue blocking and puckering work best when the harp is moved from end to end in an arc, rather than straight across the mouth. This reduces the distance that you have to move the harp in a jump. Remember—move the harp, not your head, except maybe when you're doing a shake.

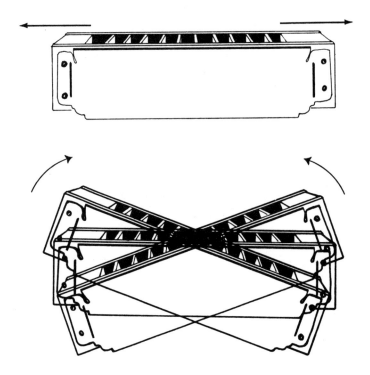

In playing any kind of music, tongue blocking makes it easier and quicker to switch from one kind of texture (3rds, single notes, octaves, etc.) to another.

To learn tongue blocking technique, start by trying to get a clear single note with a block, first from one side and then from the other side of your mouth. Once you can do that, try playing scales, first out of one side, then the other. Then alternating the notes of a rising or falling scale with a fixed note:

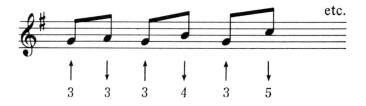

Next alternate the notes of a scale in two different octaves:

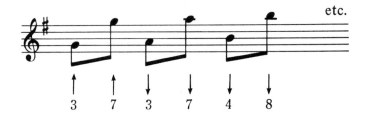

Bluegrass fiddle tunes make good practise material for this style. Check out "Devil's Dream":

Once you think you've got the basics down, you can start working out standards and jazz tunes. Ellington's "Caravan," Gillespie's "Salt Peanuts," Kenny Dorham's "Blue Bossa," and Gershwin's "I'll Build A Stairway To Paradise" all have melodies with big jumps in them, as do literally thousands of other standards. It won't do you any good to play a million notes if nobody can hear them clearly. Some people think that you can get a louder tone with a pucker than with a block. That's probably because unskilled tongue blockers are apt to pinch the corners of the mouth, cutting the volume. I'm pretty sure that Little Walter used a block, and it would be hard to play much louder than he did.

In classical music, where articulation is everything, check out each piece carefully to find out where to shift your tongue block from one side of the mouth to the other. A tongue shift can happen at any point where the reeds involved aren't side by side on the harp.

The following examples are from the first movement of J. S. Bach's B minor flute sonata. I've labelled the notes "L" (play out of the left side) or "R" (play out of the right side) to show some possible solutions to these passages.

In this style, notes are separated by *lipping*—making a quick opening and closing motion with the lips, rather than with your tongue or throat.

In the double-stop section of the chromatic harp exercises, the fourth exercise can be played as follows:

1. tongue to right, play out of left side
2. tongue centered, outer notes play
3. tongue to left, play out of right side
4. tongue centered

91

Tongue Blocking and Puckering: Pros and Cons

There are certain disadvantages to tongue blocking. Lipping can't give you the hard separation that you get when you touch your tongue to your palate. Overblowing (more about that later) also seems to be easier with a pucker. The block has to be abandoned for flutter-tonguing and the chorded rhythm work that blues players use.

Toots Thielemans and Stevie Wonder, probably the two best jazz harp men recording today, both play with a pucker. Both these men have a lot to say, and they say it well. Still, both tend towards the use of runs, or lines that travel in one direction, rather than the more indirect, circling motions that jazz horn players use. Wonder especially relies on repeated notes and stepwise motion in his solos.

Tongue shifts may be easier to use in classical music, where you can plan them, than in jazz, where you are constantly improvising. Larry Adler, a master tongue-blocker, used mostly stepwise motion in his solos on the 1938 session he played with Django Reinhardt. So the problem of planning tongue shifts while improvising at high speeds may be too much for even the best players. But don't let that stop you from trying.

Limits to Harmonica Technique

It's doubtful that any harp player, no matter how talented, will ever be able to play as rapidly as a good sax player until the harmonica itself has been drastically redesigned. Toots himself once said that it would be a big mistake to try to play the harp the way John Coltrane played the tenor sax. Compare both these men's recordings of "Giant Steps," and you'll see what he meant. Even if good tongue blocking technique could solve the problem of playing legato over large intervals, there's still the even more difficult problem of rapid breathing. Sax players can blow one long breath, wiggle their finger, and play a million notes. Harp players have to change their breathing from in to out almost every time they move. You don't have to be Jimmy the Greek to know that the odds are heavily with the sax player in a race. The only solution would be a harp that could play any pitch with either a blow or draw breath.

Until such a harp is created, the harp player's bag of tricks will remain filled more with tone ideas than supersonic licks. That's not so bad, of course, because the harp can really make some amazing sounds. Twentieth-century western musicians have played around with a lot of unusual techniques, and have learned a few things from the complex musical cultures of Africa and the rest of the Third World. If you've heard any Stravinsky, Varèse, Cage, Mingus, Coleman Hawkins, etc., you know that unusual or limited sounds can be invaluable to the modern musician. In the hope that composers and players will find a catalog of offbeat techniques interesting, I'll set down a few exotic facts about Marine Band and chromatic harps.

Avant-Garde Techniques for Marine Band

Some of the strongest sounds a harp can produce are only possible on the diatonics. The dynamic range of a Marine Band is much wider than that of most chroms. A good player should learn just how much volume he can get out of any given reed. I find that the most powerful tone on a C blues harp is the overblow on the blow 6 reed.

Overblowing is done the same way as a bend in the upper register: Tighten the jaw, bring the tongue up slightly if you pucker, and try to make the reed pop to the harmonic. Once the overblow comes in, you can lean on it hard. Midrange diatonics will overblow on the blow 4, 5, and 6 reeds—on a C harp, the overblown pitches are E♭, F♯, and B♭, respectively. Next loudest are the blow 7-10 reeds, and then the first 6 draw reeds. High range blues harps (like F) are loudest in the midrange draw reeds: low harps (like G) are loudest on the high blow reeds. In all keys, a hard pull on the draw 1 reed will make the reed go slightly sharp, often buzzing as well. Naturally, you don't want to make sounds like that on a soft, sensitive ballad.

A bend that rapidly alternates between the straight and bent pitches gives the reed a sound like a synthesizer with a rapid and deep vibrato, especially when the hands are used to swell the tone. This works best on the draw 2-4 and 6 reeds and blow 7-9 reeds. On the high reeds, the sound is truly startling, especially when you move from one reed to another.

Many blues players sometimes sing and play the harp simultaneously. Sonny Terry's fox chases are a good example. I've experimented with singing a note in unison with low register blow reeds. The sound is like Tibetan prayer chants. You can also play a full chord on the lower blow reeds, doubling the bass notes with voice, for a huge organ sound.

The small size of the blues harp makes it possible for a player with a wide mouth to stretch two octaves or more. (At last your big mouth will be good for something besides getting you in trouble.) 6ths, 10ths, 12ths, and other intervals can be played in a variety of patterns, along with very fat chords. It's also possible to play independent melodies simultaneously, but since both voices have to be either blow or draw at any given point there's a limit to what you can do. You can't, for instance, play a B against a C on a C harp.

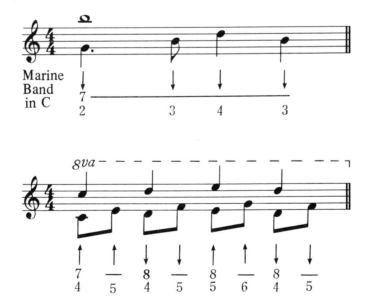

93

Special Tunings for Marine Band

The absence of certain chromatic pitches on the Marine Band (which is by definition a diatonic instrument) does not hinder the blues player, but can give the jazz player some real headaches. This problem is especially bad in the middle octaves, where a player working in second position has to do without the minor third (on a C harp in second position, Bb), minor 6th (Eb), and major 7th (F♯), all of which are very important to all jazz since bebop.

Overblowing can overcome this problem to some extent, but the overblown pitches aren't always easy to pop in. The only really reliable overblow on most harps is the overblow on blow 6 (Bb on the C harp), which leaves the minor 6th and major 7th still out of reach.

Several players have experimented with filing the reeds on the Marine Band in order to retune the harp, making these notes available. Charlie McCoy, for instance, files the draw 5 reed (on a C harp, F natural) up a half step to get the major 7th in second position. Filing is done on the end of the reed farthest from the rivet that holds the reed down. The filed reed can be bent down a half step to get the flat 7th (the original pitch).

The tuning makes it much easier to play all sorts of jazz licks in the middle register. Let's take a look at a passage from the Charlie Christian solo transcribed in this book.

At measure twenty-one, Christian plays this line:

There is no major 7th (in C, B natural) on the Marine Band, so the line must be altered:

With the filed draw 5 reed, the passage can be played with only slight changes:

Take a look at this lick from Dizzy Gillespie's "Groovin' High":

This line can be played in the middle register with an overblow on the blow 5 reed,

but it isn't easy. With the altered draw 5 reed, it's a snap:

For blues, the unaltered Marine Band is still tops, but the altered harp is good for tunes where you need to do some heavy chording on the V chord because the filed reed gives you its major 3rd.

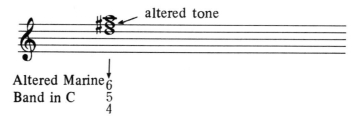

I've experimented in the past with filing the draw 4 and 6 reeds on the Marine Band a half step sharp. This is most useful on the draw 6 reed, where the space created by filing the reed can be filled with bends:

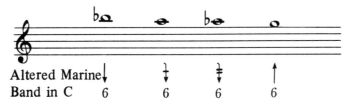

On the draw 4 reed, the advantage of gaining the minor sixth (on the C harp, E♭) is offset by the fact that you have to bend to get the natural fifth, which in second position should be a very strong note.

Overall, the most useful alteration is filing the draw 5 reed. Filing the draw 6 reed and overblowing the blow 6 reed will give you the same note (on the C harp, B♭). Since the overblow is fairly reliable on the blow 6 reed, I wouldn't bother with filing. Because neither filing the draw 4 reed nor overblowing the blow 4 reed is perfectly satisfying, I'd leave the reed alone and use the overblow when necessary. It's the lesser of the two evils.

Avant-Garde Techniques for Chromatic

Chromatic harps are not, in general, as loud as the diatonics, and they can't be played as hard. However, they are capable of some striking effects that Marine Bands can't touch.

The high register of a chromatic can be forced into overblowing easily—many players do it just by tonguing too hard—and those harmonics go way up high. If you're in a scholarly mood sometime, dear reader, you can chart out all those high harmonics for posterity. In the meantime, fool around and get used to the eerie, dog-whistle sound of the overblows.

The loudest way to play a chrom is to take the mouthpiece off a 64. You get great volume, but it's not easy to play complicated melodies. A lot of tone clusters are possible. These qualities make the stripped harp good for free music and pieces in the style of the modern composer Penderecki. A similar effect can be had by playing a normal chrom with the slides halfway in. Toots does this on Joanne Brackeen's "Snooze," off his *Captured Alive* album. This setup is more versatile, but is not as loud as the stripped harp.

The slide on a chrom (especially the CBH, which has a light, fast slide) can be used to trill single notes or chords, which can be strung together in modal blocks and melodies. The modes will all be based on a C♯ major scale. This sound is very string-like—the effect is reminiscent of some of Béla Bartók's string music. You can bend the trill, just as you bend a single note, so that it can be played through a full chromatic scale.

The harmonica has only a short history. Efforts to create a virtuoso harp tradition are more recent, and the history of the harp in jazz is even shorter. It's exciting that so little has been done so far, because there is still lots of room for exploration, maybe more than all of us can use in our lifetimes. I hope that you will try to learn as much as possible about what has been done—by the great blues men and women, jazz players, and classical players—and use that knowledge as a springboard for the creation of *new* sounds by means of hands, voice, mouth, tongue, lungs, heart, and harp. Play on!

Notes on the Exercises

Pat Martino, one of the best jazz guitarists in the world today, said in a recent interview in *Guitar Player* magazine that he never practises exercises—he only practises to hear how a given piece of music would sound played perfectly. I think that everyone reaches that point sooner or later, and once you do, exercises aren't any more fun than they are useful. While you're still learning the fundamentals though, scales, arpeggios, and other technical exercises are a big help. If you find that the technical problems of the pieces in this book are hanging you up, then you should spend at least twenty to thirty minutes a day warming up with some exercises. Then when you have to jump from a half step bend on draw 3 to blow 9 five times in a half second, you won't be applying for unemployment.

The Marine Band exercises in this book are designed to make the player more familiar with the whole harp, from top to bottom. Some of them, like the scale exercises in the sections on the Harmonicats and Tom Scott, aren't too hard once you've run through them a few times. The arpeggios and extensions are trickier because they involve a lot of jumps and changes of direction. Practise everything slowly until you know it cold, then speed it up gradually. A metronome is nice for keeping your time steady while you gradually increase your speed. Play *clean.*

The breathing exercises are designed to get you used to breathing in and out quickly with a variety of harp movements. Again, do them slowly and evenly, speeding up gradually when you have the control.

The double-stop 6ths are just one example of the things you can do with chords on the Marine Band. Try out 3rds, 10ths, octaves, and so on, using different shapes and patterns to keep you on your toes.

Try playing these exercises with different accents. For instance, if you have groups of four sixteenth notes, try accenting the first note in each group, then the second, etc. This will increase your control in fast, tricky passages. In fact, it's just about the only way to make a passage with a continuous stream of notes sound musical.

A good breathing exercise is to start a note very quietly; gradually bring up the volume for a slow eight beats until you're playing as loudly as you can; then bring it down again for another eight beats until you're barely whispering. You can also hold a note absolutely steady, at either high or low volume, for as long as you can. Remember—breathe from your gut for a deep, full sound with plenty of staying power.

The exercises for chromatic are limited to scales, arpeggios, and a few patterns and double stops. Once you know your scales, you can work out on extensions, and the exercises on 3rds, 4ths, 6ths, etc. in the Marine Band section. Transpose up or down an octave on the chrom by adding or subtracting four from the hole number. Always play your scales and arpeggios through at least two octaves, and accent to shape groups of notes and keep your rhythm even.

In the bibliography, you'll find exercise books for other instruments listed. I especially like Joseph Viola's book of patterns for sax. They're tough on the harp, but they really teach you to get around, so they're worth a go. To play jazz, you can't think note by note—it's too slow—so memorizing lots of different patterns in all twelve keys can be helpful.

Part of practising is listening. Listen when you walk, listen when you sit, and listen especially when you're playing with other people. No one is a bigger drag than the person who can't bother to listen to the people with whom he or she is playing. Listen to the music inside your head, and try to play what you hear there, even if you fumble at first. You'll never be an improviser if you don't have the courage to play your own music.

Playing jazz is hard work, but if you keep your ears and heart open you'll learn new things all the time, and you'll get there. Good luck. In the meantime,

> Man, please your maker and be merry,
> and give not for this world a cherry.

Marine Band Exercises

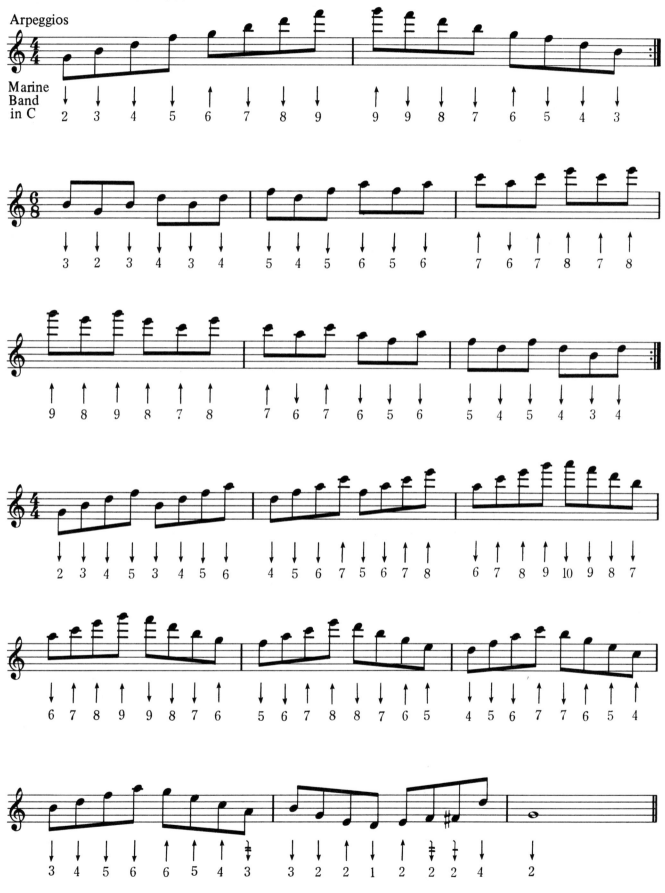

99

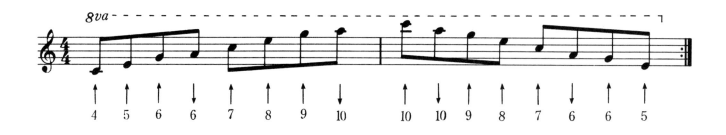

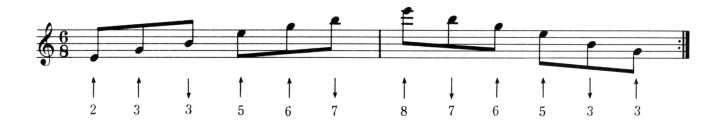

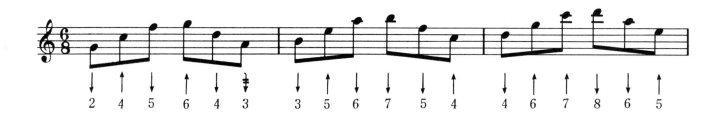

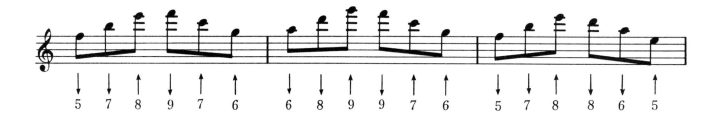

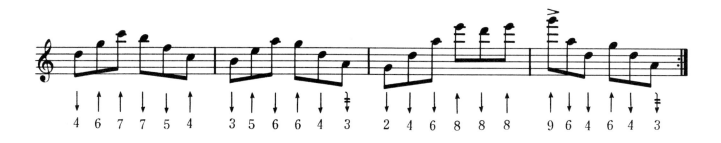

Overblows

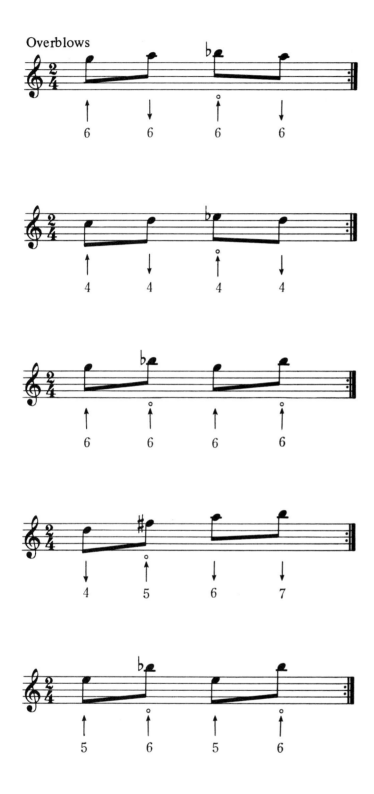

Fourths

etc.

etc.

etc.

Extensions

Sixths

 etc.

 etc.

 etc.

Sixths in double stops

Breathing exercises

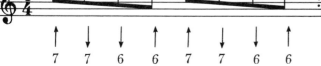

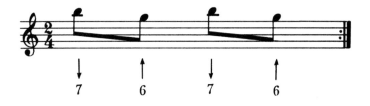

Chromatic-Harp Exercises

Double stops

Scales - major and harmonic minor

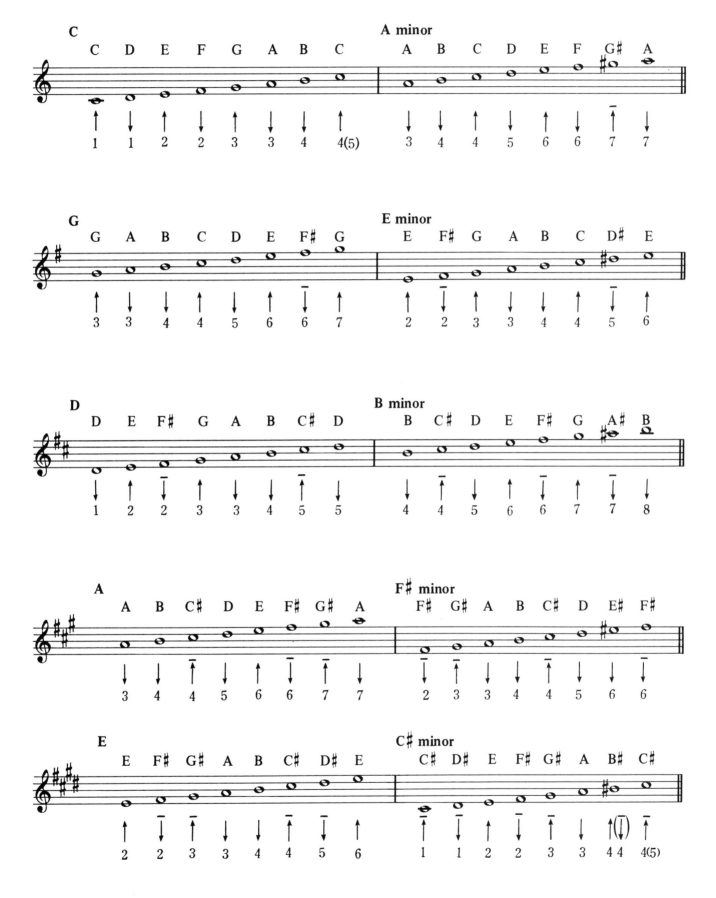

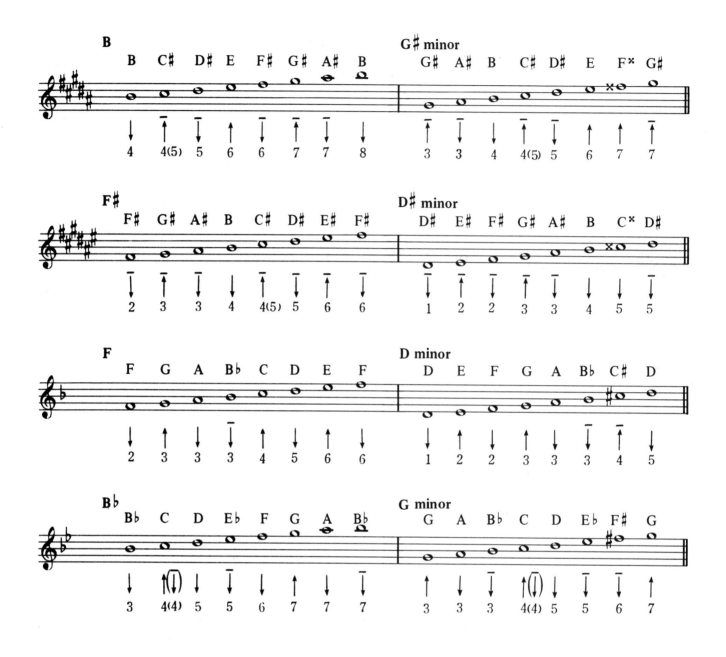

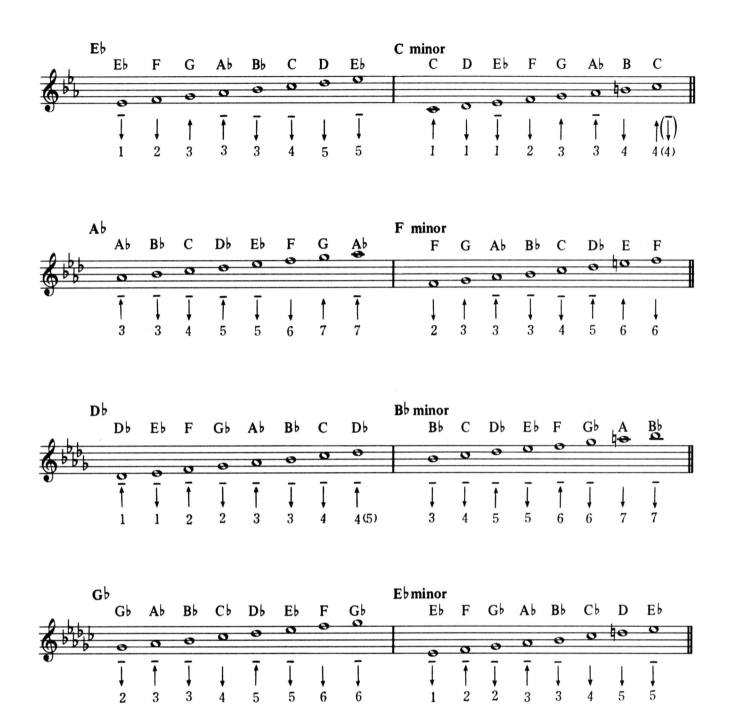

111

Arpeggios

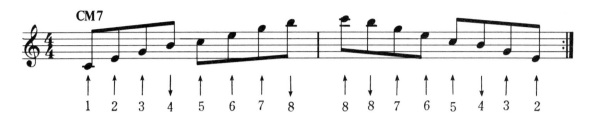

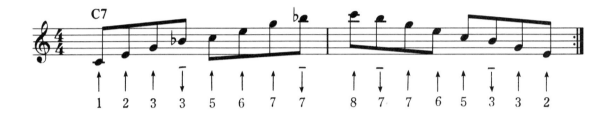

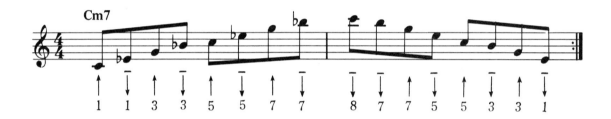

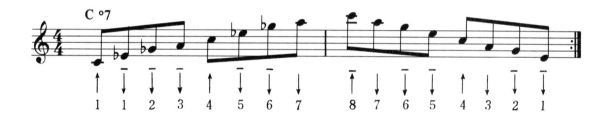

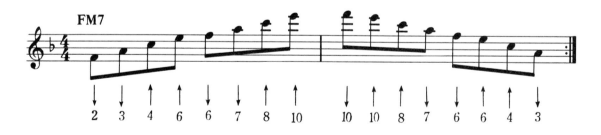

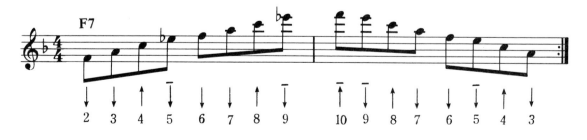

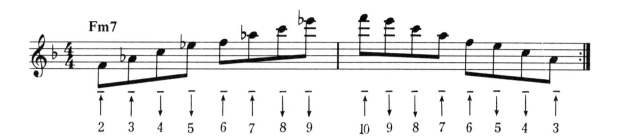

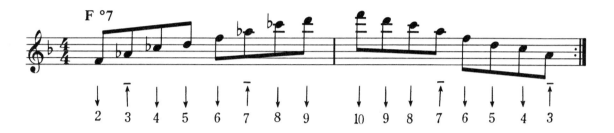

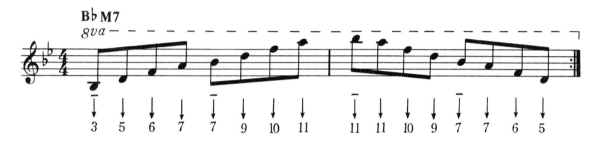

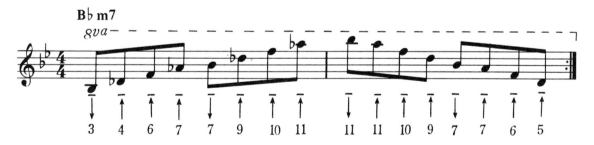

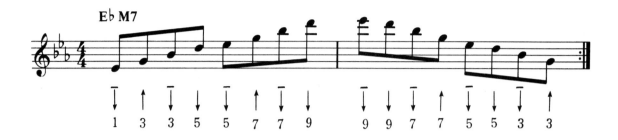

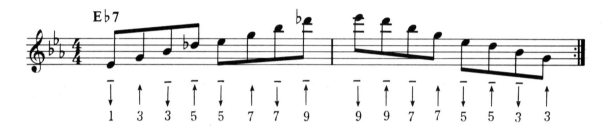

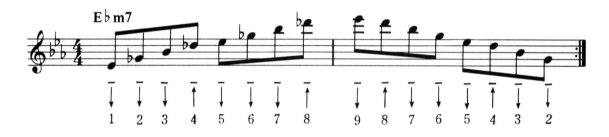

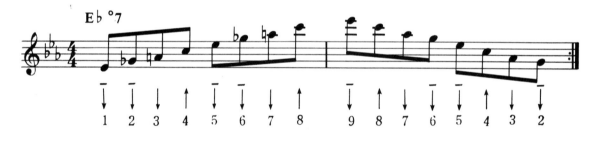

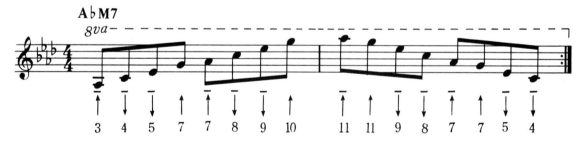

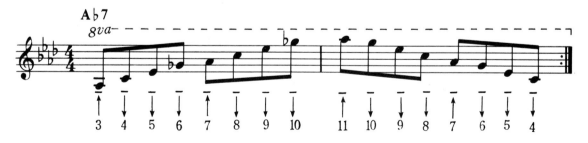

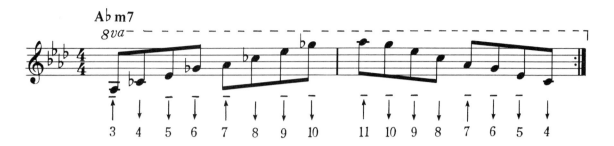

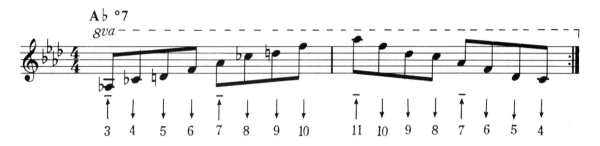

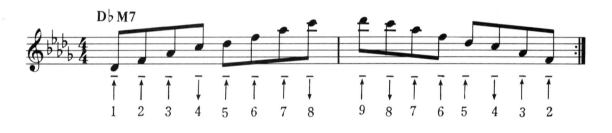

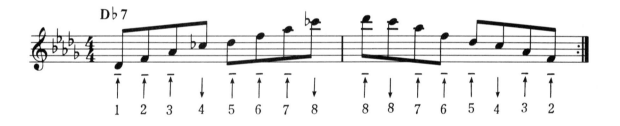

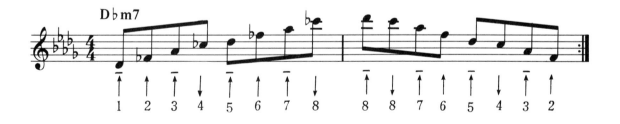

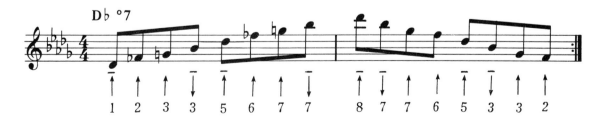

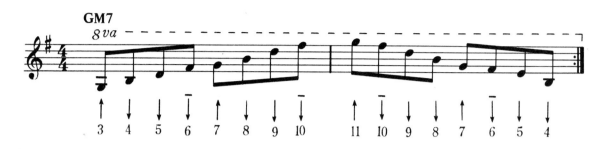

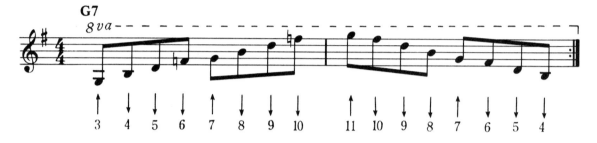

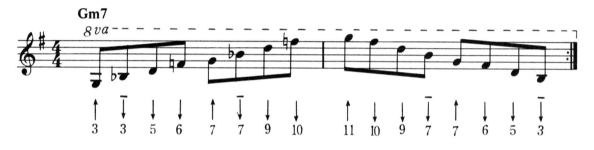

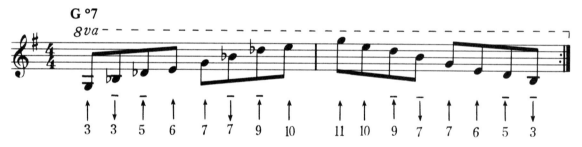

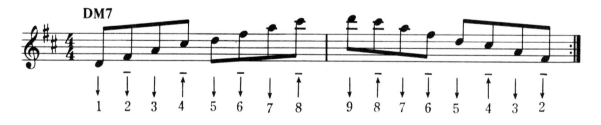

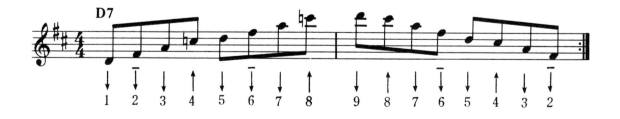

Dm7

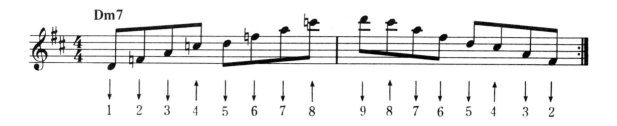

D °7

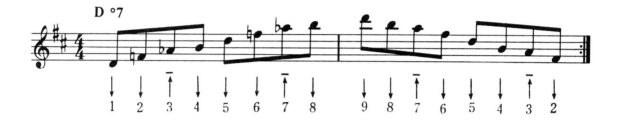

AM7

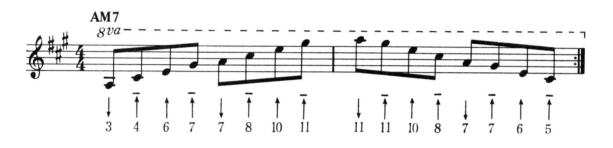

A7

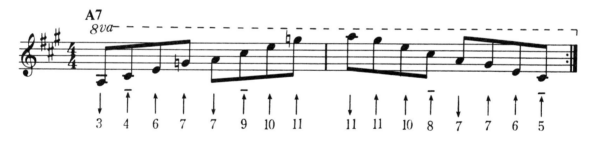

Am7

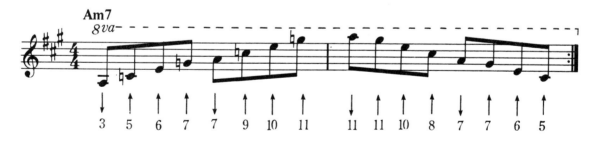

A °7

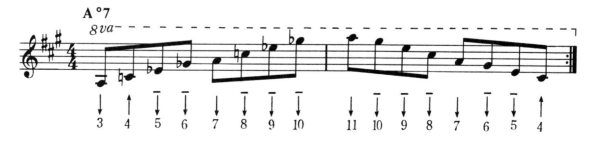

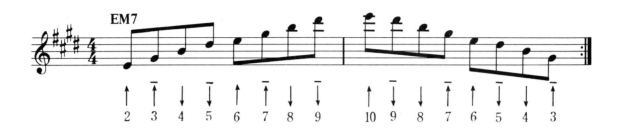

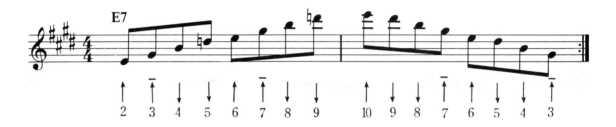

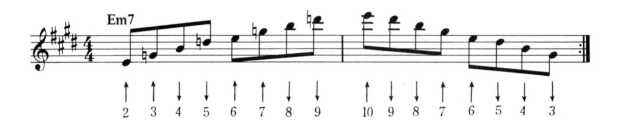

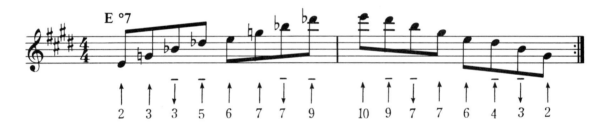

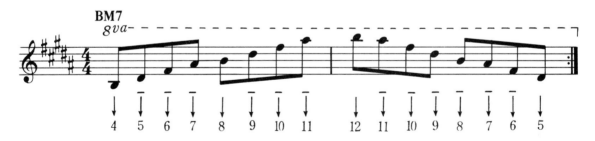

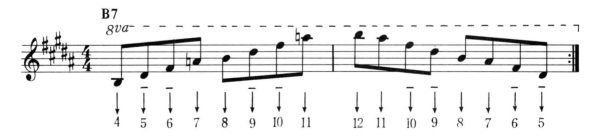

Bm7

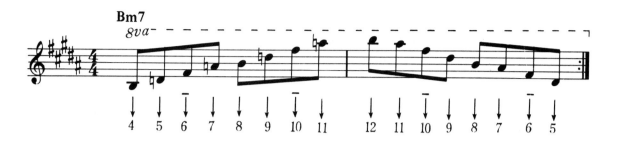

B °7

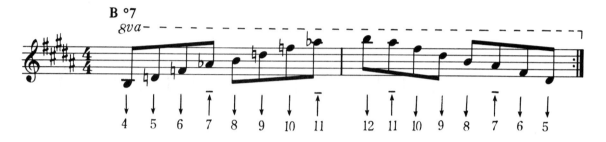

F#M7

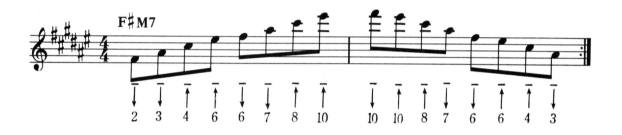

F# 7

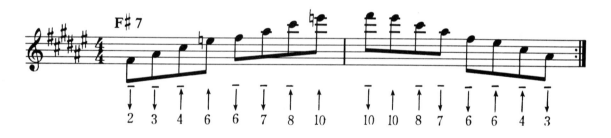

F#m7

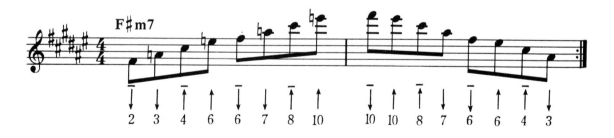

F# °7

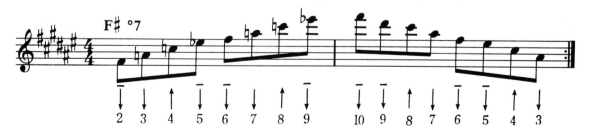

Whole tone scales

Augmented triads

Diminished scales

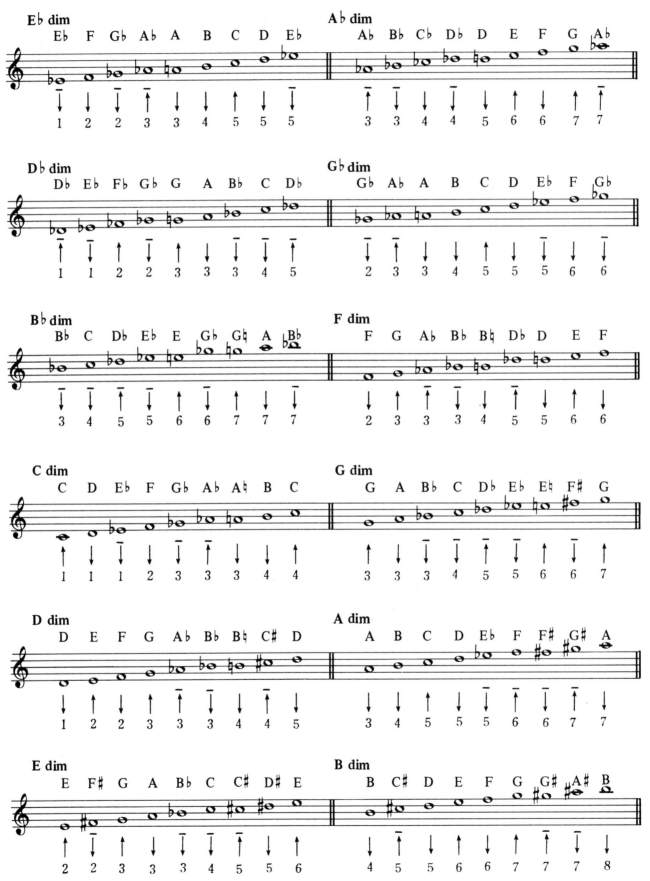

An Interview
with Toots Thielemans

Jean "Toots" Thielemans is the best jazz harmonica player recording today (and has been for the last 25 years). His style represents the most convincing compromise between the technical limitations of the chromatic harp and the demands of modern jazz. This interview was conducted in April 1979.

Richard Hunter: Before we get into anything else, there's something I've always been curious about. One of your earliest recordings with George Shearing's band was a harmonica version of "Body and Soul." Were you influenced at all by the 1938 Larry Adler/Django Reinhardt recording of that piece?

Toots Thielemans: No. Larry Adler really brought the harmonica to my attention; my jazz education was influenced by Django, of course, but even more so by Charlie Parker at that time, around 1952.

R: You've mentioned in several places that you're a great admirer of tenor saxophonist John Coltrane. You've recorded "Giant Steps" with Joanne Brackeen on piano. How do you translate Coltrane to the harmonica?

T: I didn't learn specific licks from Coltrane, like his fast runs or his wide interval leaps. You can't play that stuff on the harmonica; it sounds choppy. What I learned from Coltrane was a kind of grammar—scales, phrasing, rhythms, that kind of thing.

R: That brings up the question of what the technical limits of the harmonica might be.

T: Well, you can't get a good legato out of the harmonica when you're playing fast. In fact, for me it's a struggle to get a good tone out of the chromatic at all. I wish I could get the same sound out of the chromatic that the blues guys get out of the Marine Band.

R: The Koch harmonica has something of that sound, doesn't it?

T: A little. Listen to those blues guys though, they *wail.* Hohner sure didn't design the harmonica to sound like that.

   With the harmonica, it's hard to get past the "Look, Ma" stage, where you're showing off, to get to the point where you're saying something. The blues guys say something—that's the funkiest stuff in the world, man.

   Another thing about the chromatic is that it's a lot harder to play in certain keys than others. A run that's not too bad on a B♭ 7 chord might be impossible on a C7 chord.

R: Do you ever use a chromatic tuned to any key besides C?

T: No. I like the sound and range of the C chromatic. The G, for instance, sounds unclear in the bottom octave, and it doesn't have a top end like the C.

   The easiest way to play the harmonica is to stick to the keys where you can use mostly either draw or blow notes, and use the slide a lot. That way you can get a good legato and accenting.

R: Do you think it's worthwhile for harp players to try to play Charlie Parker heads and solos?

T: No, I don't think so. Maybe for medium tempo stuff. At high tempos you'd never get the accenting right. It's another "Look, Ma" situation—it doesn't come off.

R: If it's so hard to play things like Parker on the harp, do you think the harp can ever be a major jazz instrument?

T: Sure. Look at the trombone. That's a very tough horn to play jazz on, but when the right guys came along it happened. The same thing could happen with the harp. Of course the harmonica isn't as versatile as the tenor sax, but so what?

Every instrument does some things very easily, and some things poorly. When I worked on the *Smackwater Jack* album with Quincy Jones, at one point they transcribed one of my solos and gave it to the violinist Harry Lookofsky to play. The solo was fine for the harp, but Lookofsky couldn't play it on the violin with the same accents and feeling. And this is a guy who can read and play practically anything: So I think that any instrument has limitations, and the harmonica isn't any worse off than most. When the right players come along, it'll happen; I've done a few things myself.

The main thing is that you have to play the things that sound good on the instrument, and not try to do the things that don't come off right. You can't do a smooth trill from a blow to a draw note, for instance. There are real physical limits to how fast and smooth you can play that kind of thing.

I think Stevie Wonder is one guy who knows what sounds good. He can get around in a few different keys, too.

R: He plays a lot in F♯, doesn't he?

T: Yes, that's a good key for his style. "Isn't She Lovely" is in E—that's a good one.

R: Wonder plays Marine Band, too.

T: He does?

R: "Boogie On Reggae Woman" has a first position Marine Band solo.

T: I like that, too. I don't fool around with the Marine Band much.

R: There seems to be a real split between the classical players on the one hand and the blues and jazz players on the other over technique. The classical players use a tongue block, shifting from one side of the mouth to the other for jumps, while the jazz and blues players use a pucker to get their single notes. Do you think there's any advantage to a jazz player in using the tongue-blocking style? It might help in those Coltrane style interval leaps, for example.

T: I don't know. I've never tried that.

R: Adler uses that technique, doesn't he?

T: I would say Larry and I have a rather different approach to tone production, which may result in phrasing differences.

R: Of course you're a much better jazz player than Adler, but he is a virtuoso, and he's one of the few classical types who's ever tried to play jazz, so I thought maybe a comparison might be useful.

T: Blackie Shackner uses that tongue blocking thing, too—he's a good player. I've never tried it though, so I can't say.

R: What instruments do you prefer to use? Most photos of you show you with a 12-hole chromatic.

T: I like the 12-hole. Lately I've been using the Super 64 a lot. That has a nice sound.

R: Do you think it might help reduce the technical limits of the chromatic if a different tuning scheme were used? Say, for instance, that the chromatic was set up so that the blow scale was a C whole tone scale, the draw scale a C♯ whole tone, and pushing the slide in would give you the reverse. Then any pitch could be played either draw or blow. Would that make fast runs easier?

T: Some things would be easier. The things that are easy now wouldn't be. The chording wouldn't be the same at all. I don't know if you'd gain anything by doing that.

R: What do you think is your best work on record to date?

T: I like my recording of "You Got It Bad Girl" with Quincy Jones. I solo in F and A♭ on that tune, which at the time was a first.

I've just recorded an album with Bill Evans, the pianist, for Warner Brothers. I've been waiting for a long time for an opportunity to record with a performer of Bill's musical magnitude. There are parts of that record where the interplay between us is just fantastic. That album should be out soon.

R: Is there anything you'd like to say in closing?

T: It's good that you're being careful with this stuff. The harmonica deserves it.

Bibliography

Some of the sources listed here are quite advanced, but are still worth looking at. The complexity and variety of modern music is awesome, and any good musician, no matter what he or she likes to play, should be aware of what other musicians are doing.

Jazz History

Ross Russell *Bird Lives!* Charter House
   Maybe the best biography of Charlie Parker to date. Lots of information on the swing and bebop eras.

Martin Williams *The Jazz Tradition* New American Library
   Articles on many of the best jazz musicians. The edition I read covered up to the mid-1960s.

Journal Of Jazz Studies Rutgers University
   This quarterly magazine has excellent articles on jazz history, discographies, sociology, and musical analysis. The Summer '77 issue had a great analysis of Charlie Parker's style. The Fall-Winter '78 issue has an excellent analysis of Little Walter's style, complete with a transcription of "Teenage Beat," by that renowned harp scholar, Richard Hunter.

Ralph Gleason *Celebrating the Duke* Delta Press
   This book has won a couple of awards, and offers a very valuable and insightful look into the lives and music of a number of great jazz men and women.

Jazz Technique

John Mehegan *Jazz Improvisation,* Vols. 1-4, Amsco Music Publishing Company
   Volume 1 identifies the sixty scale-tone 7th chords, gives the modes that go with each chord, shows a few voicings, a Coleman Hawkins transcription, and so on. Volume 2 has many transcriptions of great solos. Volumes 3 and 4 discuss jazz piano styles from the 1920s to the present. Anyone interested in piano music and hip voicings should check it out.

William Russo *Jazz Composition and Arranging* University of Chicago Press
   This book covers its subject as thoroughly as can be. It'll take you a long time to get through it, but when you're ready, this is the one. A workbook has just been published to supplement this title.

Jerry Coker *Patterns for Jazz*
David Baker and Harry Miedma *Jazz Styles and Analysis for Alto Sax*
David Baker and Harry Miedma *Jazz Styles and Analysis for Trombone*
Charlie Parker Originals
   These books are all available from Jamey Aebersold, 1211 Aebersold Drive, New Albany, Indiana, 47150 (ask for his catalogue). The first book is a real aid to learning to think in groups of notes and patterns. Baker and Miedma's books are full of great solos, well worth looking at. The Parker tunes are *absolutely required knowledge* for serious jazz players.

Joseph Viola *The Technique of the Saxophone* Berklee Press Publications
   Plenty of excellent exercises on a variety of chord patterns.

Stan Ayeroff	*Django Reinhardt*
	Charlie Christian
	Benny Goodman
Charley Gerard	*Sonny Rollins*
Stuart Isacoff	*Miles Davis*
	Charlie Parker
	Thelonious Monk
Clifford Safane	*Bud Powell*

These are the titles currently available in the *Jazz Masters* series (Consolidated Music Publishers). They all have good analysis and lots of fine transcriptions.

Classical Styles and Techniques

M. Clementi *Gradus ad Parnassum*

This has been the classic text for counterpoint studies for hundreds of years.

1000 Fiddle Tunes M. M. Cole Publishing Co.

Good for breathing practise, and learning to control your tone at fast tempos. Usually played in first position on the Marine Band; play in twelve keys on the chrom.

Béla Bartók *Mikrokosmos*, Vols. 1-6, Boosey and Hawkes

The first volumes especially have many pieces that translate well to the harp (or two harps), and all volumes demonstrate a virtual catalogue of 20th-century composing techniques.

J. S. Bach	*Inventions* (two-part and three-part)
	The Well Tempered Clavier
	Notebook for Anna Madgalena Bach
	Flute Sonatas (B minor and E♭ major)

The last can be played on the chrom, although it's not easy. All of these pieces should be tried on the chrom, and listened to for a taste of what the best counterpoint sounds like.

Ludwig van Beethoven *String Quartets* (complete) Dover Press

These are about as difficult as they come, but I understand Larry Adler has played them, so that means it can be done (and maybe we should all try). This is some of the most complicated and beautiful music ever written. Approach with caution but without fear.

The Art and Technique of Harmonica Playing

Tommy Morgan *Chromatic Harmonica* Warner Bros. Pub.

This book is an excellent introduction to chromatic harp technique. It also has good info on the bass and 48 chord.

Alan "Blackie" Shackner *Everything You Always Wanted to Know About the Blues Harp and Marine Band* Warner Bros. Pub.

This book has good info on the six positions, the best chapter on repairs that I've seen anywhere, and other good stuff. I don't agree with Shackner when he says you have to learn first position before you start playing blues.

| Tony Glover | *Blues Harp* |
| | *Blues Harp Songbook* Oak Publications |

These books are fairly basic, and both are very useful for fundamentals. Oak also publishes a fine book on Sonny Terry, and will soon have books on rock and Chicago harp styles.

James Cotton and Charlie McCoy *Master Class* Oak Publications

This combination of a booklet, transcriptions, and an hour-long cassette will be available later this year, and is worth whatever they'll charge for it. McCoy and Cotton discuss and play a variety of techniques, including bending, special tunings, tonguing, and lots of other great things.

Discography

Albums Used for the Transcriptions

Joni Mitchell *Court and Spark* Asylum 7E-1001
  Lots of great music, and Tom Scott's solo on "Raised on Robbery."
The Fabulous Rhinestones *Freewheelin'* Just Sunshine JSS-9
  Available in many cutout bins. Toots solos on "What Becomes of Your Life."
Miles Davis *Kind of Blue* Columbia CS8163
  One of the best jazz albums ever. A great band, and simply constructed, brilliantly played tunes.
Richard Johnson *Plum Island* Fretless 110
  Two tunes feature harp by Mike Turk.
The Harmonicats *Harmonica Boogie*
  Latest release of this tune was in 1962, on Wing SRW16133. Collectors should have it.
King Curtis *Everybody's Talkin'* Atco SD33-385
  Out of print, but available in many cutout bins, and through collectors. Great R&B sax throughout (sounds like a harp on "You're The One").
Stevie Wonder *Fulfillingness' First Finale* Tamla 6-332
  Two of the Wonder transcriptions in this book are from this album. "For Once in My Life" will be available from dealers in singles and oldies.
Louis Armstrong with Earl Hines Columbia CL853
  Great jazz by the first great jazz trumpeter.
Charlie Christian *Solo Flight* Columbia CG-30779
  Lots of fine guitar work by Christian, and good stuff from the likes of Benny Goodman, Lionel Hampton, etc.

A Few Harp Albums of Uncommon Interest

Djangologie, Vol. 8 French EMI Pathe C-54-16008
  This album includes Larry Adler's great session with Django Reinhardt and Stephane Grappelli. It's one of the first jazz harp albums, and it has some very hot stuff on it.
Chess *Blues Masters* Series
Vol. II *Little Walter* Chess 2ACMB-202
Vol. III *Muddy Waters* Chess 2ACMB-203
  Little Walter's best stuff as sideman and leader.
Sonny Boy Williamson with Big Joe Williams Blues Classics 21
  Williamson does amazing things with his tone.
Charlie McCoy *The Real McCoy* Monument 231329
  One of the best albums by one of the best country players.
Big Walter Horton with Carey Bell Alligator 4702
  Walter has played better, but this is still very good. Lots of subtle tone control.
George Fields *Hip Pocket Bach* Angel s-36067
  Inventions, preludes, fugues, etc. on the harp—chrom and bass. Too much reverb in the mix for my taste, but the playing is excellent.